The Liberated Heart

Rosemary Haughton

THE LIBERATED HEART

Transactional Analysis in Religious Experience

BL
53
.H35

A CROSSROAD BOOK
THE SEABURY PRESS, NEW YORK

The Seabury Press
815 Second Avenue
New York, N.Y. 10017

ACKNOWLEDGMENTS
See page 193, which constitutes an extension of this copyright page.

Copyright © 1974 by The Seabury Press, Inc.
Designed by Lynn Braswell
Printed in the United States of America

LIBRARY OF CONGRESS CATALOGING IN PUBLICATION DATA
Haughton, Rosemary.
   The liberated heart.

   "A Crossroad book."
   1. Psychology, Religious.   2. Transactional
analysis.   I. Title.
BL53.H35   200'.19   74-18271
ISBN 0-8164-1167-0

Contents

Introduction

ONE of the most common and most comforting beliefs of the antireligious is that religious people will not grow up, that they want to be comforted, told what to do, protected from reality by the promise of reward in another life if in this one things are not too good. There is considerable truth to this assumption. According to still another one, religious persons are censorious kill-joys, always ferreting out sin in others, and even in themselves. They wallow in guilt and want others to do likewise. Again, the picture is not altogether false.

On the other hand, there are the saints, those men and women whose love of God made them into such lovers of men, and incidentally into such startlingly whole, mature, and glowing human beings that the human race has never been able to forget them. There was Elizabeth of Thuringia, for instance, who shocked her husband's rich relations by running around in a dirty old dress nursing the poor. Seeing the misery of the oppressed, she instituted the first food boycott in history by refusing to eat any foods

obtained from the poor by "unjust means." Since most of
the food of the rich fell into this category, her health was
permanently damaged. Thomas More, Chancellor of England and Renaissance scholar, humanist and wit, beloved
friend and family man, died rather than abandon his beliefs. And Elizabeth Fry, Quaker wife and mother, who
went into the filthy prisons of the early nineteenth century, not only comforted and helped the prisoners but
stirred up such a fuss about what she had witnessed that
she forced the government to act. More recently, there was
Franz Jägerstätter, the Austrian farmer, happily married
and the father of children, who, alone in his village (alone
among millions of "good Christians," too), refused to serve
in the Nazi army, and died for his steadfastness. And a
Polish priest who took the place of another man in the
death cells at Auschwitz, because that man had a wife and
he had not, went to his death singing.

These are a few whom events made famous. There are
thousands upon thousands that no one has heard of except
the people whose lives were transformed by their love.
It is true they constitute only a minute proportion of the
human race and a very small proportion of professing
Christians. On the other hand, they seem to have made a
remarkably good job of being human. If they had been
asked what made their lives so radiant, so purposeful, so
adult and complete, they would have said that it was God
(if they had time to attend to such a question, being normally too occupied in loving God and other people to analyze the situation).

If they are right, what is the difference between them
and those other God-people, the heavenly thumb suckers
and holy inquisitors? More importantly (since the stereo-
types of religious horrors are really comic-strip characters,
not real people), what makes the difference between the
saints and the rather pathetic, good, but ineffective and
evasive people who really do believe in God, but never
seem to leave a mark? Are the great ones just great any-

way, and is religion really only a prop for the inadequate? Or are the saints right, and is love of God, after all, *the* thing that makes a human being whole and free and really human?

These are big questions, yet the answers to them are found by observing and studying quite little things. The way people react to small annoyances, or to sudden challenges, the way they make choices of career, their attitudes toward marriage, parents, and government, toward Blacks and Whites, superiors and inferiors, are the things that reveal a person's spiritual state. And these are the things this book is about. In the course of it I hope to discover the ways in which spiritual development can mean growing toward wholeness (which means holiness). And so, of course, it is very largely about how this can go wrong, how the religious development, which should flower into a generous and radiant maturity, can get arrested and turn into bigotry or morbid self-absorption, into moral blackmail or weak evasion of responsibility, or into an excuse for hatred and cruelty.

The tool to be used here is based on certain principles of transactional analysis, which has caught the imagination of the public since the publication of Thomas Harris' *I'm O.K., You're O.K.*, but began earlier with the more sophisticated work of Eric Berne. Like most discoveries, it is one of those basically simple ideas which, once thought of, causes people to say "Of course—it's obvious!" And as is the case with any new discovery, previously unnoticed signs begin to be seen at every turn.

Also, like other valuable discoveries, this one grew out of a long process of previous discoveries and inquiry to which many have contributed. Just as, once Pasteur had identified certain bacilli, it became clear that scientists and doctors before him had *almost* found the answer (or perhaps *had* found it without realizing it), so the principles of transactional analysis, once grasped, leap from the pages of works by many earlier psychologists, educa-

tionists, and philosophers, who, however, failed to bring it
to the precision of definition that is needed if ideas are to
be really useful. And that is what matters. For a method is
needed that can be used not only by therapists and professional educators (religious and others), but also by ordinary people who want to understand themselves and their
world and do something about what they have understood.
Transactional analysis is such a method: not the only one,
nor even the best (if there is such a thing), but a valuable
one for many people.

This book is about life and its meaning and what we can
do about helping it to grow properly. It is therefore the
biggest possible subject. But because it *is* so big, it is necessary to be very precise, and careful, and to avoid vague
ideas that sound wonderful but do not really provide any
useful pointers for action. For this reason, a method such
as transactional analysis is helpful. It is precise, it is clear,
it is far-reaching but not generalized. It is a tool, and only
a tool, for finding the answers, but it is a good one—sharp,
well-balanced, satisfying to use, and carefully designed for
the job it has to do. For the same reason, however, the subject transcends the tool. Transactional analysis will not get
us to heaven nor bring peace to the world or even to a family, but it will show us what we have to do and what we
cannot do, and what, after that, God does.

Before we can use a tool we have to learn how it works.
The rest of this introduction is, therefore, a short account
of what is meant by transactional analysis. It must perforce
be brief, and the method of applying it will naturally become more evident in the course of the book. All the same,
it is essential reading, and anybody who skips this may not
get far with the rest of the book.

Transactional analysis theory rests in part on what is
believed to be a biological fact; namely that each of us
have in our brains the equivalent of a continuous tape
recording of every conscious impression, from birth and
probably before. What we actually remember is very little

and very selective, but it is all there, available for "replay" if properly stimulated. What stimulates it, as we all know, are odd things like the scent of a flower that grew in a garden unvisited for twenty years, or getting an old coat out of a trunk in the attic, or encountering a situation resembling another, long forgotten. For instance, for many years I could not stand the smell of eau de cologne, and could not imagine why. One day I was reminded that, at the age of six, I had my appendix out. In order to reassure me before the anaesthetic (in those days chloroform on a mask) the kind doctor "chloroformed" my teddy bear by putting over his nose a handkerchief soaked in eau de cologne. Ever after, the smell of cologne brought with it emotions of fear, anger, frustration, for in spite of the doctor's good intentions I was not reassured and struggled against the mask until overcome by the chloroform. This kind of memory is recorded for ever on the personal "tape" and can be recalled by circumstances. This particular memory is of the type called the "Child" recording (C.). This record runs from birth or before up to the age of about five or six, and much of it is preverbal. It consists of recordings of the child's reactions to events and experiences—mostly emotional ones, of course, though later ones will include words that try to express those feelings. The earliest ones, purely feeling ones, may be the strongest, for a baby's emotions are very strong, all the more because he has no way of understanding or controlling either the events that happen or his feelings about them. When I was six, I could understand what was happening, but the outrageous nature of what was done to me (being held down and having an evil-smelling mask clamped over my face) produced feelings of fear and rage very much like those of the baby who has literally no power to order his own life and is helpless in the hands of the grown-up people.

But of course the little child's own feelings are not all he is aware of. There are also the voices of the Giants and Ogres or maybe of the Fairy Godmothers—the grown-ups,

especially the parents, and most especially Mother. These
people have the power and majesty, they can kill or cure,
comfort or reject. From them comes food, warmth, cud-
dling, and love, or slaps, frowns, rejections, punishment.
Their voices say, "You are a darling," and the child is in
paradise, or "You disgusting little pest," and the child is in
hell. There is no appeal against their judgment. They are
Fate, Destiny, God. And they know everything. They
know how life is to be lived. They utter such maxims as,
"Always brush your teeth," "You must be polite to visitors," "God loves you," "God will punish you," "The
cops'll get you," "You'll turn out like Uncle Fred," "You
were born under a lucky star," "Men have all the fun,"
"Women are stronger than men," "Watch out, they'll get
you." And so on. These are the Laws of the Medes and
Persians, immutable, inscribed in stone, and, more importantly, recorded for ever on the "Parent" tape (P.). Most of
the time this record naturally runs parallel to the "Child"
tape, though there can be experiences recorded in the
"Child" which have nothing to do with the actual parents.
It is likely, though, that the child will associate these with
his parents. A small child who burns himself accidentally,
for instance, will regard the burn as a punishment inflicted
by his mother who said to him, "If you touch the iron, it
will hurt you!" And even if the parents are far off (for instance, if the child falls while playing with other children)
he will link this in his mind with his parents. "Perhaps
I've been naughty," he will say to himself, assuming that
this is another punishment.

The inevitable result of being very small and helpless,
always doing the wrong thing (puddles on the floor,
dropped food, tactless remarks to touchy relations) and
being under the rule of those huge, watchful people, the
Parents, who have unlimited power and wisdom, is to
make the child feel "not O.K." The only way to feel
"O.K." is to do what "they" command—and even then the
possibilities of failure or mistake are enormous. And, be-

cause the Parent knows everything, including the future, he gives the "not O.K." child his "script"—the plan for his future. The Parent says, "You'll be a doctor like your father," or "You'll end up in jail, you're just like your father," or "Our family are all subject to chest complaints," or "You can't do anything without money," or "The world is so wonderful, you're lucky to be alive!" And the Child accepts his fate. Not instantly, of course, but over years of hearing the same type of remark and injunction, telling him in a thousand ways that he is a loser or a winner.

It seems as if the human person were the helpless victim of his early years, his future and his character dictated to him before he is able to understand. All through life, as circumstances stimulate one bit or other of the "tape" to play back, the hapless grown-up will find himself reacting according to patterns laid down long before. The famous scholar, accustomed to deliver lectures to packed halls, may turn pink and stammer when he meets a dominating woman. (His mother used to say "I can't understand you! Do talk properly! You're just stupid.") The young married woman, happy and busy, will begin to look askance at her husband, watch his mail, and go through his pockets. (Her mother told her "Men are all alike, once they've got you they'll cheat, and you'll never know till he slips up!") Or the crippled, impoverished clerk whom everyone pities may be always cheerful, full of jokes and plans. (His mother said to him, "Our family never gives in! There's always someone worse off, and anyway, life is wonderful!")

Are we programmed for life in those early years, generation after generation, for ever and ever? Are we forever "not O.K.," helpless, a sick joke of the gods of chance? The determinist philosophy believes this and bids us to accept it and be happy by manipulating ourselves and each other to fit our circumstances better. There are experiments on animals of "reinforcement" techniques to demonstrate how this works. Reward a rat with enough food pellets and he will learn to operate complicated machinery. Bribe a human being with enough comfort-giving and pleasant experiences and he will run the social machine in such a way as to get them. It is true, of course, but it is not the whole truth.

The other bit of truth, the one that makes the vital difference, is the development of a third "member" of the developing mind. This is called the "Adult" (A.). It is the right name for it, although it begins to appear about the tenth month after birth, for it is the way of thinking that eventually enables the individual to grow up and make decisions—yes, make decisions. Another name for one aspect of this is "reason." It means the power to observe, compare, draw conclusions on the basis of what is known, and make decisions accordingly. The baby of a year, limited though his experiences are, can already do this. When I eat all my pudding, he notices, Mother is pleased. So if I want to please her, I eat my pudding. When Mother is pleased, she kisses me. I like to be kissed, so if I want to be kissed, I must eat my pudding. Strictly logical, very useful.

It is not always so simple for the baby, however. He sees Father give Mother some flowers. Mother laughs and is pleased and kisses Father. So logical baby goes and gathers some of the best flowers in the garden and brings them to Mother. Instead of laughing and kissing him, Mother cries out: "Oh dear, you naughty boy!" She may even smack him. At two years old, the reason for the difference is impossible to discern. The logical conclusion is "She doesn't like me, I'm not O.K." Then he cries, so Mother, repentant, comforts him. He likes this, but what he concludes is: "I mustn't do like Father, I must cry— i.e.—be a baby." This is often the beginning of a habit of retreating into Childish (C.) behavior in times of stress or uncertainty, because then, maybe, the Parent in other people will give comfort and reassurance. All the same, uneven and worrying as the process may be, the Adult continues to grow, and to make more and wider observations, and draw more far-reaching conclusions, and make decisions.

The Adult is, or should be, the well-informed reason that can both appreciate and distinguish the good and bad in his own Child and Parent. He can see if the Child feelings really have anything to do with the present situation. For instance, if a grown person feels paralyzingly shy when faced with an interview, is this feeling really due to the awe-inspiring majesty of the interviewer or to his own abysmal ignorance and weakness—or is the interviewer a normal human being, and the applicant's own qualifications and knowledge well up to the required standards? Are the feelings simply the "recording" of little Tim's feelings when faced with a new, huge schoolmaster, an all-powerful and angry Jove (maybe he had indigestion that morning, but Tim could not know that). The Adult can also judge whether the Parent recordings are really as absolutely valid and eternal as they sounded in the mind of the three-year-old. Are "the old ways" always "best" when they can be seen to produce poverty and injustice? On the other hand, if the Parental command "think of others first" seems to lead to discomfort and to contrast with the successes of more selfish people, does this prove it was untrue? Or is there some other dimension to the situation?

The Adult has to decide. It is easy to say this, but the Adult is under strong pressure from the Child and the Parent (who after all got there first), and often they can distort the evidence, making the conclusion come out wrong. So the Parent will take care only to notice the bits in the newspaper that show how corrupt politicians are, thus supporting a conclusion that "politics are dirty," regardless of any evidence to the contrary. This makes the Child feel good, because he has done what the Parent told him to do, and continued to hold that "politics are dirty." If the strug-

gling Adult enters a feeble "yes—but . . ." it is quickly
squashed. Prejudice (which is Parent on the loose) is very
powerful, and it "contaminates" the Adult.

So does the Child, sometimes. If a girl has always been
taught that women are "intuitive," incapable of reasoning,
volatile and inferior, she will also have learned by her own
experience that her "inferior" (not O.K.) Child can get its
own way by the means that children use—cajoling, tears,
petting, acting helpless. It works; the Parent in the men
she meets responds to this. The Adult in the girl concludes
this is the way things are, this is how women are *meant* to
be—and she is right, in a way, because all the evidence
supports this conclusion. And this Adult (but distorted)
conclusion reinforces the Child pattern of behavior and
causes her to pass it on to her own children in the form of
Parent precepts: "We women have our own ways of getting what we want!" "Of course I'm only a woman, but—,"
"I just *know!*," and "Aren't men beasts!"

These are a few of the difficulties under which the
emerging Adult labors. But the "contamination" of the
Adult by the Parent or the Child does not mean the Adult
cannot work. It can and does, though it needs educating, it
needs confidence. This is what books about Child Psychology, and Personal Development are really for (if they are
good). They help the person to tell the true from the false
in himself, to make real and realistic judgments on *all* the
available evidence, and decide accordingly.

People who are lucky in their parents have an easier
time, because their Parent recording will tell them real,
useful, and flexible things, things of permanent moral and
practical value. For them, much of what their Parent says
reinforces and supports the Adult, and sets it free to make
right decisions. So the mother who tells her child "Don't
be rushed into things, make up your own mind," and lives
up to that herself, is giving the child's Adult an enormous
advantage. The father who says (and lives by) such a philosophy as "It's the quality of life that counts, not how big

your income is," is providing an intelligent and hopeful future for his children. Even the best parents have their failings, and the one who says, and means, that "It's what people are, not what they have, that counts," may also have a violently expressed dislike of people who "borrow" cigarettes, and a weakness for expensive restaurants (and for those who take him there). But the contradiction will prove unimportant, probably, because the Adult in his children, given permission to judge by real and lasting standards, will distinguish the trivial from the fundamental even in their own Parent recording.

The general structure of the mind's efforts to cope with reality is now reasonably clear, expressed in the code P (Parent), A (Adult), and C (Child). P.A.C. becomes, therefore, a code way of describing the ways people react to each other, and so a way of helping them to react more constructively and realistically. This is "transactional analysis," the analysis of the type (P.A. or C.) of statements or questions, and the responses to them.

Here is a personal example. A few days ago, my youngest daughter (aged five) came home from school in a bad temper. "We had a *horrible* pudding for dinner," she said. She said it in a whiny voice, pouting and dragging her feet. She leaned against the table and dropped her bag on the floor. All these signs made it clear that her "Child" was talking. She felt aggrieved and wanted a good moan and some sympathy.

There were three possible ways for me to react. One was Parent: "Don't be silly, take off your coat, pick up your bag, and stop fussing about nothing." I could have enforced the second and third, but the first and fourth are meaningless commands, and anyway the exchange would have got us nowhere, because *her* reaction would have been either tears-and-lying-on-the-floor (Child) or angry arguments (Parent, as far as she is able to reproduce it!). Either way we would have ended with a row and a spoiled afternoon. Another way I could have reacted was the one she wanted—Child to her Child: "Poor darling, how horrid for you, here's a goodie to make up for it!" This would certainly have led to future whining and complaints, the first being so successful. The third possible response was Adult, something like this: "That's bad luck, but I expect it'll be a nice one tomorrow. Did you do any painting today?" or something similar. The idea of this is to get the child's Adult working, to judge the *real* situation, put it in its place (i.e., "unimportant") and get on to something interesting. If that works, the child responds with, "Yes, I did a lovely picture of a zoo, with two elephants (etc. etc.)." This (successful) transaction would then be expressed thus:

C. I had a horrible pudding, etc.

A. Bad luck, but it'll be nice tomorrow, etc.

A. I did a lovely picture, etc.

You can tell at once when the child changes from Child to Adult. The slurred, whining voice changes to crisp, clear speech, the pout gives way to smiles and bright eyes, the body becomes upright and alert. People express the changes in different ways, but once you are on the lookout it is not hard to spot them. Parent, for instance, has the frown, the loud, smug voice, the stamped foot or pounded table, the gaze that sees not another human being but an object of propaganda. Child is more varied, because Child experiences may lead to anxious tightness of muscles before the unpredictable threat, or coy undulations to seduce the dangerous grown-up. But the "spaniel" look, the lowered face, the pout, the high wavery voice are usual Child signs. The Adult, on the other hand, is generally relaxed but alert, speaks in a moderate tone, and uses phrases like "I think," or "let's try," rather than "All X's are Y" (Parent) or "I can't" (Child).

However, life is not as tidy as all that. Anyone who wants to apply P.A.C. will have to realize that a lot of the evidence is unspoken and has to be guessed from experience of the person or the possibilities of the situation. The reason why, in some cases, trained therapists come into the picture is that people become so tangled up by the fears and rages of their Child and Parent that they are afraid to let the Adult take over, in case he offends the Parent or hurts the Child. And many people, knowing this, instinctively concentrate on comforting the Child and placating the Parent, rather than making an attempt to activate the Adult. In any case, the Child often needs to be comforted. (Doctor Harris calls this "stroking," to link it with the comfort of physical holding and petting that is literally a condition of survival for the baby. Babies, unhandled, pine and die.) The comforted Child is then reassured and willing to let his Adult have his say. In the same way, the anxious and strict Parent has to be kept quiet and calm, at least until the Adult is strong enough to tackle him directly.

In the little example I gave, therefore, none of the replies I suggested were any use by themselves, not even the Adult one, because the little girl was tired and edgy, as yet unused to the many experiences of school, and—as always—ready for a fight if contradicted. Knowing this, I could not reach her Adult directly. Fortunately, I was not (as I might have been) harassed and Parentish at the time, or feeling sorry for myself, so I was able to be Adult in my assessment, i.e., my internal reaction was neither "She's got to learn to put up with things" (P.), nor "As if I hadn't got a headache already, and all this ironing, without a scene from her!" (C.). So I had to keep her Parent quiet, by avoiding any feeling that she was being contradicted, and I had to comfort the overwrought, tired Child, before I could get the Adult to work. And fortunately this is not hard when the subject is only five. So what actually happened was apparently illogical, for I ignored the actual remark, knowing it was really only a symptom of general resentment at a world too big to understand and cope with. Instead, I took off her coat and remarked, "How cold your hands are." We washed them in warm water, then she sat on my lap and we had a little cuddle. By that time, her Parent had gone to sleep and the Child was feeling happy and definitely "O.K." So then I said, "That was bad luck you didn't like the pudding, but I expect there'll be a better one tomorrow. Did you do any paintings?" And soon I had a description not only of her own painting but of every other painting in the class.

In fact, after about ten minutes she told me (looking rather sheepish) that the pudding had really been very good ("Jelly and *cream*")! So we laughed about that, and it was then that I explained (even though she is only five) *why* she had told me a silly lie, and how she would perhaps do better next time. Our particular version of P.A.C. is, as a matter of fact, known privately to the two of us as Bossy Emma (P.), Big Emma (A.), and Baby Emma (C.), all easily identifiable by Emma herself.

I have given this little example from my own experience in some detail, not because it is "typical" but because it is from thousands of such unmemorable incidents that a person's life and future is built.

I could quote many more dramatic examples, some happy, and some sad from the present and the past. There is the little girl whose father had habitually molested her sexually from the age of five, though she never told because of his threats: "You're no good," he told her, by word and act, "You're a bad girl." So she set out to become a bad girl. At every moment of stress she reacted with panic, guilt and fear, alternating with fits of futile rage and hate directed at all grown-ups. With one family she was quiet, cheerful, Adult in a tentative and unformed way, feeling for a way out of her prison of guilt and despair. It is a toss-up whether the Adult will grow stronger or be swamped by the vicious Parent and the terrified, hopeless Child. There was another little girl, unloved and neglected at home, who was told at school "God loves you." The message got through. By that one statement she confounded the "not O.K." verdict of human beings, and grew up a confident, able, and loving woman. Yet, when she had a son, she was so afraid to lose the unusual comfort of human love that she spoiled him atrociously. Her Adult ran her life, and set her free, but her unsatisfied Child interfered effectively with the Adult in that one department.

This brings me to the end of this introduction and acts as a bridge to the rest of the book. The attempt of P.A.C. analysis is to help people to realize that they can decide, they can change, because, all their Child feelings notwithstanding, human beings "are O.K." There is Hope, and there is Love. This is what Christianity is about. You may feel not O.K., and behave not O.K., and in fact be not O.K. in all kinds of real and important ways. But somewhere in you is the O.K. person, the one God is creating in his own image, if only a little cooperation is offered. So there is Hope, and there is Love, if you have Faith.

1

"Lord, That I May See!"

THE human child, from the moment of birth, is at the mercy of the grown-up world, with all its fears and anxieties, its efforts and hopes and loves and failures. Though he does not understand them, he is touched by them and his unfolding consciousness is shaped by them. Yet this helpless human thing, so Christians believe, is capable of the vision of God, of utter fulfillment in freedom and love. Clearly, the way reality is mediated to the infant by his particular grown-ups will make all the difference to how, and even whether, he reaches any notion of that staggering invitation to eternal life. Christian attitudes to children have come in for a lot of criticism, and rightly so. Sometimes it seems that children perceive God (and often do not call Him that) in spite of, rather than because of, religious teaching. Does this mean that the best policy is "hands off the children"? Or do we owe it to them, in spite of all the mistakes we are likely to make, to try to convey to them some idea of the tremendous vision which is the Christian Gospel: the risen Christ, the living

1

statement that freedom, hope, eternal life, are not just pac-
ifiers to keep the masses quiet.

When the baby emerges from the womb he begins his
Quest, the great journey on which all human beings set
out. He does not know anything, yet he has within him the
power to know the All. What is his destiny? Wholeness?
Eternal life? Nirvana? Heaven? The goal of the Quest has
many names and many symbols. The Holy City, the Well
of the Water of Life, the Bird of Paradise, the Back of the
North Wind—lovely names. In tales and sayings, human
beings remind each other that there is more to life than
dishes and commuter train, bills and neighbor's gossip.
And they pass this awareness on to their children in fairy
tales and songs. Only very often they do not know what
they are saying.

Still, however cynical we may become, there is still that
odd longing. For what? We try to pin it down to a better
job, a new car, a holiday, only when we get them we still
want—Paradise. The Quest, we feel deep down, has still
to be undertaken. Some of us stifle the feeling. You can
tell by the faces: grim, smug, slightly frantic, but hard.
Hard, so as not to let nostalgia, hope, love, take hold. But
that hope survives in the grimmest circumstances.

Mr. K. lived in a rotting slum house in a big city. He was
dying. He had a "not very bright" wife and a big family.
The walls were cracked and damp, and the children
kicked the door of the outdoor lavatory before they went
in—to scare away the rats. In summer, Mr. K. had his bed
moved to the window wall, though it was the dampest,
because then he could look out. What he saw was a narrow
strip of yard, a water tap, the outhouse, the gasworks
beyond. When a friend painted up the driest room (it had a
big hole in the floor) for the younger children, the family
celebrated the great event. Mr. K. ran the household. His
wife could not count, so she would bring him the change
from the loaf of bread, the pint of milk, and he counted it,
to make sure she was not cheated. He paid the rent on
time, joked with the children. One thing he wanted,

though: a canary! "I used to breed them once," he said.

Why a canary? Would a canary cure his mortal disease or secure a future for his "simple" wife and their children when he was gone? Would a canary mend the roof or soften the landlord's heart? No, a canary can only sing. It is only a yellow symbol of hope. To Mr. K., a canary meant that this is *not* all there is—somewhere, somehow, there is another world; there is God. He did not spell it out, perhaps he did not even believe in God. Did he get his canary? I don't know. In any case, he passed to his children a message that life is *good,* worth living, *you are* O.K., no matter what happens.

But how did they get that message? Did it correspond to some inner knowledge that was already implanted? Or did they have to learn it "from scratch"?

This curious creature called man—so beautiful, so brutal, so sensitive, so coarse, and so obstinately alive—sets out to find the truth about himself. He does not know what he is looking for, he only knows he is blind, and he wants to see. That seems strange. How does he know he is blind? If his blindness were total he would not know there was anything to be seen. Is the notion that we lack a "sense" but that we can recover it, or discover it—is this a learned conviction (or maybe a comforting fantasy)? Or are we born with such a strange idea? The yellow canary is a symbol of that vision, the golden light of a dawning in a world which is ours but which we mostly know only by hearsay.

Are children born "innocent," and therefore somehow already in touch with God? Or, even if they are somehow basically "O.K.," is this innocence so smothered by ignorance and infant selfishness that it cannot get to work? Do little children "know" God in their inmost hearts and only require that grown-ups not interfere with this precious relationship? Or do they have to be taught to know God, in words and gestures, by moral habit, by assent to doctrine, or by "conversion"?

We really have to try to find some answers to such questions, else how can we know what to do? How, otherwise, can we tell whether our efforts to lead a child to God are helpful and truthful or merely clumsily destructive, or just plain lazy?

Many sincere and thoughtful Christians, especially parents, have been concerned about the answers to these questions, though naturally most parents have been content to accept whatever doctrine about child-nature was accepted by their time and place, and make do with that. Only a minority have questioned the "normal" idea, and they have not always done any better than their ancestors. It will be a help to see how Christians of the past tackled the problems raised by the early religious formation of children—both the practical problems and the theoretical ones, and to see how the results of their ideas are still shaping ours—thus also, of course, those of our children, through us. We are our history, and we cannot understand ourselves without seeing how we got to be what we are. And there seem to be two main views of the nature of childhood religion, as I suggested—the "age of innocence" view, and the "little sinner" view.

Is childhood a period of innocence, all too soon smothered by grown-up cares and miseries? This still popular view was that of enlightened educators of the late eighteenth century. Rousseau and other radical educational reformers thought of religion as necessarily confining and oppressive, a relic of medieval superstition. They thought of childish freedom as involving freedom from all religious ideas.

But Wordsworth and other romantics sometimes saw the child rather as God's fresh creation, still half heavenly:

> Whither is fled the visionary gleam?
> Where is it now, the glory and the dream?
> Our birth is but a sleep and forgetting;
> The Soul that rises with us, our life's Star

> Hath had elsewhere its setting,
> And cometh from afar:
> Not in entire forgetfulness,
> And not in utter nakedness,
> But trailing clouds of glory do we come
>   From God, who is our home:
> Heaven lies about us in our infancy!
> Shades of the prison house begin to close
>   Upon the growing Boy,
> But He beholds the light, and whence it
>   flows,
>   He sees it in his joy;

Wordsworth's visionary child, sadly losing the "seeing eye" as he grows, until the vision fades into "the light of common day," is one picture of childhood.

It certainly corresponds to one kind of childhood experience. Leila Berg, a school teacher with a very "seeing eye," has recorded this common little tragedy of one stage in the destruction of "innocence":

> In a bus queue, a three-year-old was talking animatedly to her mother. The mother stared ahead, silent—until suddenly she exploded, her voice furious, detonating. "That's all I ever get from you!—chatter, chatter, chatter!" The little girl's lively, intelligent face changed, and she looked away, self-conscious, off balance, and silly. I wondered what else a mother expected to get from a three-year-old. What else has a small child to give? And what gift could one have that is more tender, more joyous, more remarkable?

"You're not O.K." is the mother's verdict on the child's spontaneous pleasure in people, shops, weather. "You're not O.K., and neither are the things you think are interesting!" The world is evil, dull, hostile. Remember that. "Shades of the prison house" indeed! It was the realization of the terrible damage that adults do to children by forcing them into the chains of fear and resentment and boredom and hate, that made Blake cry out on their behalf in his poem "London," in *Songs of Experience*.

> I wander thro' each charter'd street,
> Near where the charter'd Thames doth flow,
> And mark in every face I meet
> Marks of weakness, marks of woe.
>
> In every cry of every Man
> In every Infant's cry of fear,
> In every voice, in every ban,
> The mind-forg'd manacles I hear.
>
> How the Chimney-sweeper's cry
> Every blackening Church appalls,
> And the hapless Soldier's sigh
> Runs in blood down palace walls.
>
> But most thro' midnight streets I hear
> How the youthful Harlot's curse
> Blasts the new born Infant's tear,
> And blights with plagues the Marriage hearse.

But Blake was not sentimental. He knew that the corrupted child is really corrupted, along with the society and its institutions that enforce corrupting conditions. Law ("ban"), government ("palace"), or religion (church) are all implicated, and even love becomes a corrupting corpse on its "hearse" of conventional marriage, in a society that is deaf to the abomination of child prostitution. Yet it is not only obvious horrors like these that drive men's minds to forge their own manacles, it is the little, humiliating details that convince every child that he is "not O.K." Are the "age of innocence" poets and philosophers right, then? If grown-ups have thus changed innocence to bitter experience, does the answer lie in trying to preserve that

innocence untouched? Will the child learn "I'm O.K." and
go on that way, if only we stop training him, above all
about God?

The child naturally responds to God, needing only love
and freedom to grow—that was a view of childhood religion that became increasingly popular with liberal educators, though it was a very long time before it had any effect on the religious education of the majority of children.
Yet, when it did come into its own, it somehow did not
work as well as it should have. The "innocence" of childhood seemed to require more than absence of restraint in
order to develop. This carefully untouched child mind had
a way of turning sour, and so rousing reactions of disgust
and rejection in others.

C. S. Lewis, author of the much-loved Narnia tales for
children, had a real phobia about undisciplined children,
which must surely have resulted from personal encounter
with the less happy results of extreme "liberalism" in education. Like many others, he was so disgusted by it that he
let his own Parent take over (it did so rather easily) and he
lumped together in one loathsome category the whole
"progressive" milieu that, to him, produced the spoiled,
precocious child. The story *The Voyage of the Dawn
Treader* begins with a description of the kind of child he
hated:

> There was a boy called Eustace Clarence Scrubb, and
> he almost deserved it. He didn't call his Father and
> Mother "Father" and "Mother," but Harold and Al-
> berta. They were very up-to-date and advanced peo-
> ple. They were vegetarians, non-smokers and teeto-
> tallers and wore a special kind of underclothes. . . .
> Eustace Clarence liked animals, especially beetles, if
> they were dead and pinned on a card. He liked books
> if they were books of information and had pictures of
> fat foreign children doing exercises in model schools.

Eustace Clarence's parents, it emerges, are also paci-
fists. Thus did the Parent shed discrimination and thought,
even in such a wise and witty man as Lewis, when some
unpleasant brat aroused his resentment. But the description has enough truth in it to sting, and Lewis' description
(in *The Silver Chain*) of Eustace's school is equally biased
but, again, not without a grain of truth:

> It was a . . . "mixed school," but not nearly so mixed
> as the minds of the people who ran it. These people
> had the idea that boys and girls should be allowed to
> do what they liked. And unfortunately what ten or fif-
> teen of the biggest boys and girls liked best was bully-
> ing the others. All sorts of things, horrid things, went
> on which at an ordinary school would have been
> stopped in half a term; but at this school they weren't.
> Or even if they were, the people who did them were
> not expelled or punished. The Head said they were
> interesting psychological cases—"

This is a travesty of the many attempts by great educators to bring freedom into children's lives, and let them
grow in their own way. Moreover, bullying is, alas, not
confined to "experimental" schools. But it is a needed
warning against too easily assuming that the removal of restraints is enough to make children "good" and happy.

It led, in practice, to a lot of misunderstanding and misery, because the vision and beauty of childhood was
treated as something that just was, if nobody interfered by
moralizing or punishing. The nostalgia for the lost vision
(the hope for an O.K. Child) made grown-up people load
onto real children a demand that they be that O.K. Child—
and this on the order of the Parent, with all the overtones
of guilt and obligation that that implies.

In contrast to the fictional account, here is a real-life
report from a practicing child psychologist:

We get quite a number of child patients (at the child-guidance center) who are in an acute anxiety state because there is little or no control in the home. The parents have the mistaken idea that, left to themselves, the children will gradually make order out of chaos, and establish their own moral sense. They appear to have no idea why God made the family, and why the holy Child was given a human father, to whom he was subject. A very extroverted and energetic adolescent girl once told me her parents were ardent readers of books on child psychology. They never frustrated her in any way during her infant and early junior years. If she asked whether she should do this or that, or what she should play with, she was told she must make her own decision. She perfectly well remembered the intolerable burden this placed on her, and gradually came to feel that it was because her parents did not love her that they left her so much to her own devices. Once she had the terrifying thought, "if I wanted to burn the house down they would let me; and then we should have nowhere to live." [Eve Lewis, *The Psychology of Family Religion*]

Religious educators of the "liberal" nonmoralizing kind created an ideal child because they needed it. In a competitive, sordid adult world, they, the grown-ups, wanted a reassuring vision of the ideal, innocent Child. So modern Western liberal culture has created the image it needs, a child who is full of physical and mental curiosity—creative and inventive, friendly, spontaneous, generous and sociable, ambitious (but not mean to lesser brethren), uninhibited, mischievous, a bit "sassy," yet loving and kind. And the religious educator adds to this beautiful picture a dawning but inborn awareness that God made him to be happy, and to love. But somehow, these enlightened educators feel, it is not right to tell the small child much, ei-

ther about God or about what is involved in loving people:
not yet. Time enough for that when "shades of the prison
house begin to close upon the growing child." Until then
he should be left free to enjoy life, spontaneously and
creatively. That love is difficult, and life hard, and God a
complex and easily abused concept—these things he must
not know. In fact, the doctrine of the "age of innocence,"
of "original virtue," comes up immediately against the
problem of evil. For the myth of the Naturally Good Child
might, in P.A.C. language, be expressed by saying that
Western parents and educators keep turning on a Parent
that tells the Child he *is* happy and good, God says so. So
he gets the idea it's wrong to feel "not O.K.," and if he
does, Mother and Father (and God) will be displeased. Yet
circumstances themselves, in spite of all reassurance and
help by grown-ups, will make the small child feel "not
O.K." He falls down and grazes his knee. It hurts. He cannot reach that shiny thing on the table—or he reaches it
and it is a jug of water that falls, wetting him and breaking
the jug. Even if his mother merely smiles placidly, his
plan has gone wrong, he *is* wet, the jug *is* broken, and he
feels bewildered and uncomfortable. If his mother reassures him, he soon learns to cope with such experiences.
He learns, "I'm not O.K., but with help I can be," which is
the beginning of the state of mind in which religious ideas
can grow. If, on the other hand, he gets the idea that his
parents are upset and offended when things go wrong for
him (because that makes them feel "not O.K."), he dare
not ask "Why does the fire burn me?" or "Why does
Grandma move so slowly?" because it makes the grown-
ups uncomfortable, and he senses this. When he tries to
apply his developing Adult to the problem of unhappiness
and uncertainty, and to his moral decisions, he is labeled
precocious and either frowned at or laughed at. So then he
cries, and they get fed up with him. It's all his own fault
for not being as happy as God and Daddy and Mommy say
he is.

No wonder so many young people emerge from childhood convinced that the great sin is to be unhappy. And since everyone is unhappy sometimes, they are frequently in this sinful condition.

This is a distortion of moral education, because the grown-ups are using the notion of childhood innocence not to liberate the children from the pressure of adult mistakes and hates, but to protect themselves from the facing-up to evil, as the child encounters it. Because we do not want to think about pain, old age, death, the corruption and misery of our world, we do not want to let the child recognize it, either. Thus, his Adult is prevented from making any sense out of the evil he encounters. The inevitable "not O.K." feelings created by experiences of failure and pain and humiliation are enormously increased because he feels blamed for them. To tell such a child "God is good and he loves us" only puts God among the grown-ups who are all telling him, in effect, "It's your fault if things are bad. The badness *is in you.*" No other conclusion is possible. Since neither the grown-ups nor God will admit a convincing "place" for bad experiences in the scheme of life, it must be the fault of the one who minds— the Child. In contrast, Leila Berg tells how some parents behaved when their son, aged seven, wanted to watch the TV news of a terrible disaster in a nearby village, when a coal-slide came down and engulfed the village school, killing almost all the children of the community. Hour after hour, day and night, for five days, the TV cameras recorded the digging for bodies, the weeping mothers and fathers, the little corpses being carried out, the coffins and the funerals. The child would not let the set be turned off, and meanwhile he acted out the disaster with a heap of toys and a flashlight. When he had finished, he was able to resume his normal life. His mother reported that he had an unusual ability to cope with difficulties because he had worked it all out in his own way. Those parents, with heroic restraint, suppressed their own distress and did

not, as many might have done, rush to switch off the appalling pictures to "protect the child"—but in fact themselves. This is not a panacea—there are some horrors, past
and present, from which it is indeed best to protect children until they are old enough and stable enough to cope.
But to refuse the Child the right to think about the evil
side of life is not to protect the person, it is to implant feelings of guilt.

At a more personal level, a mother of a severely cerebral-palsied child had to answer the child's "why's" about
her own condition. Through all the patient care and treatment, and the tremendous achievements in gradual control
and independence, there was pain—pain in the body, and
worse, pain in the mind, as the child watched other children run, climb, dance, set off for walks with friends. And
though she would one day, after all the years of struggle,
be independent, she would never really be "like other
girls." If you believe deeply in a God of love who made
each human being to be happy, what do you say to such a
child about the God who let her be "different"? It is worth
recording what this mother said, because her answer has
to do with the preservation of the real "age of innocence,"
the assurance that one matters, that, in spite of everything,
"I'm O.K., God says I'm O.K." It happened when the little
girl was seven. The hours and days and months and years
of strenuous exercises had borne the hoped-for fruit—the
child was able, lying on her back, knees bent, to move her
own feet in "reciprocal motion"—the first real step to independent walking and a huge triumph of patience and
hope against heavy odds, for both mother and daughter.
Perhaps it was joy at the achievement, mixed with a sense
of all the work still to be done (and memories of pain and
sleepless nights and medicines and tears) that made the
little girl, Karen, choose that afternoon to ask the crucial
question: "Why did God make me a cripple?" Here is her
mother's account of her reaction:

"Here it is," I thought, "and I'm not ready for it, after all." I breathed a quick prayer for guidance. I fully realised how much depended on my answer. I sat at the table beside her. "I think, Karen, because God loves you better than most people," I answered slowly. "He didn't pick Gloria or Marie or Rosy to be C.P. [Cerebral Palsied]; he picked you. You have suffered already and you will suffer more. Not only will your body be hurt at times, but your mind and your heart. It takes a very special person to handle hurt. . . . Karen, whom do you think God loved more than anyone else in the world?"

She pondered. "His mother, I guess."

"You're right, darling. He loved his mother more than anyone else, and yet He allowed her to suffer more than anyone else. Suffering, sweetheart, is a sign of God's special love. That's why you're crippled and we're not. He just loves you more, that's all."

"It's hard, but I'm really lucky. It's all right now I know." [M. Killilea, *Karen*]

The interesting thing about this bit of teaching is that it is both true and untrue. Theologically, God does not love some people more—but some people can "let in" more of God's love. To the extent that they can realize God's love, they realize their own lovableness, they know, "God thinks I'm O.K.," and so they open to Him. The crippled child might easily think "I'm not O.K., because I'm ill, restricted, feeble. God doesn't love me." The mother's words corrected any such feeling, and thus preserved the real innocence, which is the sense of being lovable.

But there is another side to this particular story, and it helps to show the inadequacy of the doctrine of the Naturally Good Child. We have seen how easily it can be distorted by grown-up fears and prejudices, and yet there is something there, which we can call innocence, which does indeed need to be protected and cherished. Yet it is not by any means always the people who believe most strongly in "original goodness" who are best at this cherishing. The mother of the cerebral-palsied child was a very traditional Catholic with strong notions about right and wrong and the need for punishment. A mother with more faith in a child's innate goodness might not have succeeded as she did, for she was ruthless in suppressing any hint of self-pity. Never was the Martyred Innocent (beloved of the writers of nineteenth-century tracts) allowed to gain a foothold! So, one day the child was playing "hospitals" with some little friends. Karen could not move as fast as the others, naturally, but was always encouraged to try. Her mother, called to the telephone, came back from outside the room in time to hear Karen tell another child to fetch something she wanted, adding "You have to do it for me—I'm crippled." Her mother marched in and gave her a resounding slap.

What! Hit a crippled child? Poor little thing! But "poor little thing" is the world's verdict on such children—and her mother's whole effort was directed to reversing that verdict, at least in the child's own mind, and she had a clear idea that there was a real danger of self-pity, laziness, despair. In her view, the child was *liable to sin* and needed correcting. Paradoxically, it was the believer in original sin who most successfully cherished the true innocence—the secure confidence of "God thinks I'm O.K., so you have to think so too!"

And she did. A year later, playing on the beach, some passers-by looked pityingly at Karen's crutches and braces. "You poor little thing" they said.

> "It must be awful to wear those braces—you poor child!"
> "Why?" asked Karen.
> "Why—why—well—because———."

"I'm lucky," said Karen. "You just don't understand."

They stared at her.

"You see," Karen explained patiently, "I can see
with my eyes, hear music with my ears, and I can
speak as well as anybody. Mom says better than a lot
of grown-ups . . . Goodbye."

Karen's education, in fact, was, as far as doctrine went,
in line with a much older tradition than the one we have
inherited from the eighteenth-century Enlightenment.
This is what is generally regarded as the "orthodox" Christian one, and it certainly does not accept the idea that the
child is essentially innocent and corrupted only by grown-
up lies and hatreds. On the contrary, it assumes that man is
born with evil inclinations. But this does not necessarily
mean that the mainstream Christian tradition considers the
young child sinful, in the sense that he is capable of personally doing wrong. Misunderstanding about this doctrine, and distortion of it, have impressed themselves
deeply on popular Christian and post-Christian cultures,
and since the "enlightened" rejection of religion as a
blighting and restricting influence on human life (especially child life) was due to exactly such distortions, it is
worthwhile to take a look at what the older tradition really
taught. For all modern notions about religious education,
"conservative" or "progressive" alike, have grown from
the conflict and interaction of these two main doctrines
about the child-soul. Is a child born good and becomes
evil? Or is he born evil and trained or converted to good?
Or are *both* doctrines an oversimplified attempt to understand a very complex and delicate spiritual development?

This conflict becomes a little more comprehensible if
we think of it in P.A.C. terms. The age-of-innocence view
of childhood assumes a Child who feels and is O.K. unless
grown-ups tell him otherwise. Unintended influences do
not count. Likewise, intended influences which produce

the desired results are assumed to be what the child naturally does. But there is, here, a Parent in some way mas-
querading as Child—saying, "I'm the *real* O.K. Child, be
me, and you'll feel good." The obedient Child does, and is
comforted and approved by this odd kind of Parent in himself—unless, of course, he breaks the script agreement by
being unhappy or feeling guilty!

The older tradition assumes the Child is as "not O.K." as
he feels and will become less and less O.K., both through
direct bad influences and indirect ones "inherited" by all
human beings. But the Church, which here functions as a
communal "Parent," can change all that. It can make him
O.K., by virtue of the absolute "O.K.-ness" of Christ—
through baptism. Thereafter, the Church, the Communal
Parent, will inculcate beliefs and rules of life which, if accepted, will lead to approval, both interior ("I'm O.K.")
and exterior, that is, the warm sense of public acceptance
and comfort which Doctor Harris calls "stroking."

This view of childhood had many variations, including
the extreme one that saw the "unconverted" infant as actually bad and condemned to hell fire. This extreme view
was exceptional, but the feeling that children were very
far from holy innocents was common to Christian teaching,
as it is to ordinary experience. And since most such doctrines were elaborated by men who either had no family
responsibilities or left them to women and servants, it is
not surprising that childish misbehavior was identified
with the workings of something called "original sin." Yet,
St. Augustine, always identified with a pessimistic view of
human nature and blamed for much later "puritanism,"
was in fact both realistic and ironically amused in his reflections on the "sins" of his own babyhood.

Who shall remind me of the sins of my infancy? For in
Thy sight there is none pure from sin, not even the infant whose life is but a day upon the earth. But who is
to inform me? Perhaps this or that tiny child in whom
I can see what I no longer remember myself. What

then were my sins at that age? That I wailed too
fiercely for the breast? For if today I were to make as
gluttonously and as clamorously, not of course for my
mother's breasts, but for the food I now eat, I should
be ridiculed and quite properly condemned. This
means that what I did then was in fact reprehensible,
although, since I could not understand words of
blame, neither custom nor common sense allowed me
to be blamed. . . . Surely it was not good, even at that
time, to scream for things that would have been
thoroughly bad for me? Thus, the innocence of children is in the helplessness of their bodies, rather than
in any quality of their minds. These childish tempers
are borne lightly, not because they are not faulty—but
because they will pass with the years.

The growing Adult in the child will perceive that these
are not the ways to get the comfort he really wants. And it
is true that the "helplessness of their bodies" is the reason
that small children should not be expected to conform to
grown-up standards, if we include in this concept the uncertain quality of the information a baby can get through
his senses. And if Augustine was too ready to notice infant
"wickedness," he was also able to describe with loving accuracy *why* a baby gets angry and also how love first
comes into the child's life. He sees, if only implicitly, that
it is the longing for comfort and reassurance (Harris'
"stroking") that made the baby angry and creates the first
occasions of what can be called "sin"—if we mean by that
rejection and revenge. This passage is so sensitive and so
full of gentle insight that it is worth quoting, if only to
show that the towering intellect of one of the greatest men
who molded Christian thought cannot be held responsible
for later ill-treatment of little children in the name of
Christ.

At that time I knew how to suck, how to lie quiet
when I was content, to cry when I was in pain: and

that was all I knew. Later, I added smiling to the
things I could do, first in sleep, then awake—and gradually I began to notice where I was, and the will grew
in me to make my wants known to those who might
satisfy them; but I could not, for my wants were
within me and those others were outside; nor had they
any faculty enabling them to enter into my mind. So I
would fling my arms and legs about and utter sounds,
making the few gestures in my power—these being as
apt to express my wishes as I could make them: but
they were not very apt. And when I did not get what I
wanted, either because my wishes were not clear or
the things were not good for me, I was in a rage—with
my parents, as though I had a right to their submission
. . . and I took my revenge in screams. That infants
are like this I have learned from watching other infants!

Yes, infants are like this, they do have these frustrating
experiences, long before the age when memory can help
to sort out impressions. These are the earliest "not O.K."
feelings, and they result in reactions of anger and revenge
which easily "replay" when similar stimuli occur later on.
Augustine, like most Christian teachers who gave thought
to early childhood education, assumed that children were
indeed inclined to evil, as all human beings are, but that
another spirit was equally at work in them, which with
help could overcome the evil. So all depended on teaching, both by word and example. Children were often severely punished, but for many centuries this did not do as
much psychological damage as one might expect because
there was a rough justice about it. Life was harsh and
crime was brutally punished, and children saw this all
around them as soon as they could see. Consequently,
when they became old enough to reflect on it, their own
lot did not seem too outrageous. Above all, the basic motive was generally one of justice. Punishment was inflicted

for a particular fault and that wiped out the score. So even
if the parent or teacher hurt the child in a fit of temper or
for a trifle, the victim could connect cause and effect without difficulty. The medieval handbooks for parents
stressed consistency in punishment. The young sinner
knew where he stood; his Adult had something to work on.
The conclusions he drew might be grim but at least they
were clear, and above all there was little attempt to link
punishable behavior with *sin*. The Common Parent, the
Church, taught that, whatever the bad-tempered individual
Parent might say and do and impress on the young, a child
below the age of reason was not capable of serious sin. Sin
was for grown-ups. In an age when the voice of the recorded Parent included a great deal of what the Church
taught (either through actual parents or in sermons, and so
on) this helped the emerging Adult. It did not make the
punishments less harsh, but it did make them less worrying. Sensitive children suffered, but generally grew to accept physical punishment and other kinds of pain. "Life is
like that."

To his teachers, the medieval child was neither a little
angel nor a fearful sinner. He was regarded as basically innocent though wayward, extremely ignorant, and badly in
need of teaching if he were to learn to lead a "godly, righteous and sober life" as the book of Common Prayer later
put it. If he happened to die in his early years, the contemporary religious view of essential child nature was made
unequivocally clear, for the little body was carried to the
grave with flowers and thanksgiving. The Mass vestments
at the funeral were the white of rejoicing, for this innocent
soul was being returned to God, untouched by evil. No
prayer would be said for that soul for none was needed.
But if he survived, he would be taught his religion along
with his trade or his lessons, in sermons, in precept (if he
had a good home), in the paint and glass and stone of the
churches, in music and rhyme. He might grow up bawdy
and cynical, his Adult might later reject much of the teach-

ing of the Church-Parent, but it was there as language
about life, about facts, which everyone accepted, even if
they chose to ignore it or question it, or mock the failure of
churchmen to practice what they preached.

Typical of this approach were the "precepts of living"
which, at the very point where the Middle Ages ended
and the Renaissance took over, Dean John Colet com-
posed as part of the catechism for the scholars at his new
school of St. Paul's. Here we find that matter-of-fact mixture of morality, hygiene, spirituality, and common sense
was characteristic of the medieval notion of teaching children religion:

> Love God
> Thrust down pride
> Forgive gladly
> Be sober of meat and drink
> Use honest company
> Reverence thine elders
> Trust in God's mercy
> Be always well-occupied
> Lose no time
> Falling down, despair not
> Ever take a new, fresh purpose
> Persevere constantly
> Wash clean
> Be no sluggard
> Awake quickly
> Enrich thee with virtue
> Learn diligently
> Teach that thou has learned, lovingly.

This has a very "Parent" tone, and indeed it was intended to be literally "recorded" in the minds of the
young by rote learning. Similar precepts would be drilled
into children from the very beginning, and discipline often
harshly enforced. But at its best, it was consistent and

clear. The anxious, tentative Child might fear the rod, for "The birchen twiggis be so sharp, It maketh me have a faint heart," as a schoolboy rhyme of the time said, but the mind was reassured. The Adult could cope with such notions, for they made sense. The Adult could soon feel "I'm O.K., or at least I can be if I really try!"

It takes a very self-confident culture to be as clear and straightforward as that in the approach to the religious formation of young children, and that very self-confidence could breed the horrors of persecution of the nonconformist. For good or ill, that mood has gone so far that it is virtually impossible to recapture it. It raises no echoes in modern thought about religious education, but it has much to teach us, as we shall see.

Still with us, if only negatively, is the extreme opposite to the Wordsworthian view of childhood as a period of heaven-tinged innocence and vision. This is the evangelical approach to child nature, in which the standard of judging is shifted drastically from what could be observed and seen ("wash clean—learn diligently") to the feelings, and our very "subjective" modern approach to religion is linked to that change. For the Evangelicals believed that a person could be saved from Hell only by a full, personal, conscious conversion to Christ. Good conduct was quite secondary; what mattered was first to realize one's sinful state, and then to repent and call on the Lord. But repentance and faith are not written clearly on the face and actions. How do the anxious mother and father know whether their little one is saved? The questions, the exhortations, the demands—what can these mean to a little child? Yet it matters enormously to the Child that he should discover what the Parent wants of him. Clearly, if he cannot produce what is required he will be rejected, he will receive neither comfort nor love. The terror of the small child in his situation is so keen that it is scarcely increased by the one thing he can understand in all this— the threat of external hell fire, which is vividly described.

There exist many records of Evangelical children weeping for their sins!

A girl called Catherine Corbett records:

Before I was ten years old . . . I spent many hours in secret, weeping and praying to the Lord to take me to himself. I was so much afraid of pride that I could hardly be persuaded to put on new clothes, lest they should make me think better of myself, and I had a continual fear of doing or saying anything to offend God. [P.E. Sangster, *Pity My Simplicity*]

George Whitefield, the American Evangelical, was such a powerful preacher that he even induced Benjamin Franklin, an obstinate man, to abandon a prejudice against a particular charitable cause and contribute to it. His effect on children is recorded in his own account of preaching to the children of his Orphan House:

My little orphans now begin to feel the love of Jesus Christ. . . . When we came to church, the power of the Lord came upon all. Most of the children, both boys and girls, cried bitterly . . . the congregation was drowned in tears . . . for near two hours, four or five girls have been before the Lord, weeping most bitterly. [ibid.]

On another occasion he records: "A boy about eight . . . wept as though his heart would break."

If we perceive the word "sin" as a description of the human experience of estrangement, fear, ignorance of oneself and others, and the consequent anger and malice that so readily follow, then it is not hard to believe that these children could be brought to a consciousness of sin very early and had plenty of cause to weep. And once they had learned the proper expression of repentance and faith,

how sweet the approval of the Parent must have been! No
wonder the pious Child felt happy, for both God and man
combined to tell him he was now O.K.—and what is more,
for eternity. But his Adult did not have much chance—the
data were too confusing to sort out. It was safer not to try.
And yet, some of these tormented infants grew up as
happy and well-balanced Christians. We shall need to ask,
why? And the question becomes more urgent and more
difficult when we realize that side by side with this demand for early conversion was the idea that the conscientious educator must break the child's "sinful spirit," which
meant in practice that the child was coerced by a mixture
of threats, fears, and physical punishment into total submission. This submission to the Parent was seen as a necessary proof of repentance.

Susannah Wesley, mother of John Wesley, brought up
her children on this plan and set the tone for many other
conscientious parents:

> I insist upon conquering the wills of children betimes
> [she wrote] because this is the only foundation for a
> religious education. . . . As self-will is the root of all
> sin and misery, so whatever cherishes this in children,
> insures their after-wretchedness and irreligion, and
> whatever checks and mortifies it, promotes their fu-
> ture happiness and piety. . . . Break their wills be-
> times; begin this great work before they can run alone,
> before they can speak plain, or perhaps speak at all.
> Whatever pains it costs, conquer their stubbornness
> . . . therefore 1) let a child, from a year old, be taught
> to fear the rod and to cry softly. In order to do this, 2)
> let him have nothing he cries for; absolutely nothing,
> great or small. . . . 3) At all events, from that age,
> make him do as he is bid, if you whip him ten times
> running to effect it. Let none persuade you it is cru-
> elty to do this . . . break his will now, and his soul
> will live. . . . [ibid.]

Mercifully, most parents were not strong-minded enough to carry out this program in all its vigor, for human love and common sense, as well as pity, moved in. Even young David Copperfield had his Peggotty to turn to after his stepfather had finished with him:

> "David," he said, making his lips thin by pressing them together, "if I have an obstinate horse or dog to deal with, what do you think I do?"
> "I don't know."
> "I beat him."
> I had answered in a kind of breathless whisper, but I felt, in my silence, that my breath was shorter now.
> "I make him wince, and smart. I say to myself, 'I'll conquer that fellow;' and if it were to cost him all the blood he had, I should do it."

And when he eventually does beat David for not learning his lessons properly, "being unable to remember anything but my fear"—it is the burden of guilt that is hardest to bear:

> He beat me then, as if he would have beaten me to death. . . . Then he was gone; and the door was locked outside; and I was lying, fevered and hot, and torn, and sore, and raging in my puny way, upon the floor.
> How well I recollect, when I became quiet, what an unnatural stillness seemed to reign through the whole house! How well I remember, when my smart and passion began to cool, how wicked I began to feel! . . . My stripes were sore and stiff, and made me cry afresh, when I moved; but they were nothing to the guilt I felt. It lay heavier on my breast than if I had been the most atrocious criminal, I dare say.

Dickens' wicked stepfather is a villain, and Davy hates him. If, even so, the child feels so oppressed by guilt, how much more miserable and confusing it was for children whose parents sincerely loved them but whose warped religious sense drove them to such treatment. Even a brief reading of these excesses makes clear, indeed even clearer than do the mistakes of the "age of innocence" school of thought, one thing that many modern religious teachers are inclined to ignore, and that is the fact that right doctrine is important. It is not the whole story—love and sincerity are important too, and so is reason and common sense, as we shall see. These evangelical parents were often sincere and loving. It was the doctrine, unleavened by any other considerations, that children were sinful and in danger of Hell if they did not repent, that did the damage; just as the doctrine of spontaneous infant goodness did damage of a different kind.

But fortunately this logical extreme was not always reached, and it is comforting to read a description of the family life of one of the most famous of Evangelicals, the Methodist Adam Clarke:

> When his work was finished, he would open his study door and shout: "Come all about me!" From all corners of the house the children hurried to climb on him. Then, with children climbing all over him, he would parade round and round the room. After this followed Prayers at their mother's knees, and then Clarke himself put them all to bed. A "companion in their play," he invented moral fairy tales for them, and kept supplies of tops, whips, and hoops, in exchange for which he expected some useful thing to be done. The children were not allowed to receive money from visitors and he was careful rarely to praise them directly, but his regime was liberal. So also . . . his letters . . . are homely, gentle, and affectionate. They tell of the goodness that was in him, but they do not make demands of the children. Like Charles Wesley, Adam Clarke believed in example more than precept.
> [*Pity My Simplicity*]

But there was clearly plenty of precept. This family is just as truly Evangelical as the one in which the mother "would sometimes take them by the hand, and with weeping eyes say to them, 'My dear children, I cannot be at rest until I see the work of grace begun in your heart,' " or in which little Sarah Henley would tell her younger brother and sister of their lost condition by nature, "weep over them and pray for them, that they might be converted from their sinful state." What made the difference, since the doctrine was the same, and the parents in these and similar cases may be assumed to have been loving and sincere people? The difference can be discerned by using P.A.C. The damage is done when the doctrine is applied by the Parent, that is, without any adaptation to circumstances. The type of child, his real reaction and degree of understanding—these are ignored. The doctrine is simply applied in a "pure" state, unadulterated by any Adult considerations. The same doctrine, thought over by the Adult, can be applied with happy and reasonable results, though naturally there can be mistakes here, too.

It is interesting to see how ideas of religious training can change with experience in the mind of one profoundly Christian mother. Elizabeth Fry, born into a wealthy and talented family, was a lover of gay clothes, a hater of the dull Quaker Meetings held in the local Meeting House at Goat Lane, Norwich. All the sisters kept journals, and a frequent entry was "Goats [Goat Lane Meeting House] was Dis.! [disgusting]." Elizabeth was eventually converted to being a "plain Quaker" and accepted gladly the restrictions involved, the simplicity of dress and the loss of music, theater, and other pleasures. These seemed to her to be a necessary sacrifice for the sake of her faith, which offered her so much joy, so much to do and to be. But with her own children it was different. She deeply wanted them to share her faith and her Quaker convictions, but she could not bring herself to discipline them into conformity, as more severe Friends were constantly telling her to

do. She refused to beat them or let them be beaten, however naughty they were. (And they were a very rowdy lot;
they caused her acute embarrassment by their behavior
during Meeting.)

"Much grieved, very shocked," she wrote in her journal,
". . . to overhear sad screams from poor Johnny and to
find that he had been whip'd in a manner truly unmerciful
which I stop'd, but it has left a painful remembrance."
Having been a timid child herself, her son's cries brought
it all back. But that did not stop her worrying, with reason,
for she was not naturally a "good mother." "I fear they suffer much from our not having the knack of managing
them," she wrote in her faithful journal. "I often feel very
low and try'd by it," says Elizabeth's timid Child. Another
time she notes sadly, "Dear 'Chenda [her sister Richenda,
who was not yet married] thought the children ought to
be under more subjection."

She was torn two ways. She hoped for her children to
share her vision of faith and life, and she was constantly
being told by relations and friends what she ought to do
about it. They said it was her fault (a) for not being strict
enough, and (b) for being away from home about her
prison visiting, and speaking at Meetings, which, she felt
"led" to do. (They never seemed to feel the same objec-
tion to her much more frequent absences when she was in
demand as a nurse by one of her numerous relatives.) But
Elizabeth, though troubled by this appeal to her Child,
had clear Adult principles, which she confided to her journal:

Children should be deeply impressed with the belief
that the first and great object of their education is to
follow Christ and indeed be true Christians; and those
things on which we, the Society of Friends, differ
from the world in general, should not, I think, be impressed upon them by only saying, as is often done,
"because Friends do it," but singly and simply as

things that the Christian life appears to us to require,
and that therefore they must be done. They should
also early be taught that all have not seen exactly the
same, but that there may be many equally belonging
to the church of Christ who may in other respects be
much stricter than ourselves as we are than they in
these matters.

It is typical of the Adult that (unlike the Parent, which
simply quotes, giving equal weight to all the commands) it
distinguishes what is essential from what is desirable but
not essential. Notice the typical Parent remark "because
Friends do it!" At that date, and with her depth of conviction and involvement in the Friends, this passage is an astonishing proof of her clear mind and integrity of heart. Indeed, she never did let her timid and love-craving Child
allow her to give in to the demands of others, however
much she respected them and wanted their approval and
feared their reproof. She thought it out for herself, on the
basis of good doctrine and faith and common sense, and
formulated her own conclusions, which were soundly
Christian. Years later, she managed to overcome her own
Child anxieties over her children even more thoroughly.
She never did become much good at "managing" them,
and was often either short-tempered or unwise, as when
she sent her sixteen-year-old son abroad with some friends
and a tutor, but told the poor tutor never to let them go out
alone in the evenings, "or attend any public place of
amusements," but to "retire quietly after reading a portion
of the holy Scripture"! But in the end she learned to stop
worrying, and she expressed in so many words what had
been implicit in her earlier treatment of her children. This
passage beautifully expresses her hard experience, her
careful, thoughtful faith, and above all her respect—both
felt and *thought*—for the human decision of her children.
In spite of failures of temperament and judgment (how encouraging for other parents are the failures of this great

woman) she always had guided and encouraged the Adult
in her children, reassured the Child in them by her obvious love, and made sure that what they recorded from her
in the Parent should be sensible and verifiable in later life.
Other influences, indeed, spoiled some of her work, and
most of her children left the Society of Friends. This was
mainly because of the way other Friends treated their father when he became bankrupt, and it does not detract
from her achievement:

> The longer I live, the more difficult do I see education
> to be; more particularly as it respects the religious re-
> straints that we put upon our children. To do enough
> and not too much is a most delicate and important
> point. I begin seriously to doubt whether as it respects
> the peculiar scruples of Friends, it is not better to
> leave sober-minded young persons to judge for them-
> selves. . . . I have such a fear that in so much mixing
> religion with things that are not delectable we may
> turn them from the thing itself. I see, feel, and know
> that where these scruples are adopted from principle,
> they bring a blessing with them, but where they are
> only adopted out of conformity to the views of others,
> I have very serious doubts whether they are not a
> stumbling block!

We have not come far, it seems, since Elizabeth Fry's
ruthless honesty sorted out the wheat from the chaff in her
own experience of teaching children "to follow Christ."
But perhaps we have come far enough, at least in time, to
look with some detachment at these differing views of
what children are like, and therefore how best to help
them to see, or at least look for, the ultimate things.

In doing so, these very different views of child-nature
are not merely of historical interest. We cannot look back
from our superior position and dismiss the views of our
forefathers, for our forefathers are, in greater or lesser de-

gree, our "Parent." The doctrines by which they lived, they imprinted on their children, as their own parents had done on them, and the children in turn passed on the message, down to ourselves.

The message changed, as we have seen, sometimes through "breaking the script" handed down by the Parent, when the Adult felt free to realize inconsistencies or failures in his Parent commands and beliefs. Sometimes it happened through "sticking" to the script, but in the literal way that the Child interprets it, for whom the letter of the law is all. Thus, a mother will say "Candy is bad for your teeth," meaning "so don't eat too much, and clean them afterwards," but the Child (unless his Adult corrects matters later) will hear this as a Parent doctrine—absolute and eternal. He will either refuse all candy, or he may reject the Parent by guzzling the stuff (but expecting to feel huge cavities forming within minutes). In the same way, the Church/Parent may say: "Every human child inherits the sin of Adam, and is in need of salvation." This doctrine is thought over and applied by thoughtful, observant men and women something like this:

> Every human being is, from birth, subject to outside evil influences and probably weakened by inherited tendencies in his own temperament as well as by the limitations of human knowledge. So if he is to develop as Christ promised, he will need a lot of help and guidance in order to discover for himself that freedom and full humanness which is the Gospel of Jesus.

This is not just a modern "softening" of traditional teaching, it is, in up-to-date language, the kind of thing Christian thinkers worked out from early days. It is the Adult Christian, commenting on observed events and reactions, side by side with the Gospel revelation, and drawing simple, sensible conclusions about both.

But how does the Child record such teaching? It easily

takes the form, "Children are born sinful, that means they are bad. They are bad because Adam sinned, and they inherited his sin." This is a distortion of the doctrine of "original sin," but it is the way most people think of it. And the fact of the salvation offered by Christ becomes equally distorted. It may become a Parent command, "Do as the Church says and God will say you're O.K." (and you'll feel better). This is simple, because you then go on being O.K. unless you "sin" by breaking the rules, but if you do you can be O.K. again by saying you are sorry (or confessing) and being forgiven by the Church/Parent. Or it can be an expression of the Child's need for reassurance: "God says I'm not O.K., but if I say it's my fault then God will be pleased, and he'll pretend I'm O.K. and he'll be kind to me." This, in what Eric Berne calls "Martian," is the doctrine of Justification. Either way, if the need for re-assurance is great enough, if the desire for social accep-tance is added to the inner need for "O.K.ness," then the child—and later the Child in the grown-up—will strive to "repent" so as to be accepted, to feel the comfort of *"now* God says I'm O.K." But this means denying the Adult the right to think too much about the matter—he might inter-fere and upset things. This interference used to be called "intellectual doubt" and was dealt with by "making acts of faith" in one's "O.K.ness." There was a very strong motive for doing so, and this helped to create the anti-intellectual climate of much "revivalist" religion, and also of the popu-lar Catholic piety of the nineteenth and early twentieth century. It is apparent, now, in some aspect of "charis-matic" experience and in the "Jesus people."

Because this kind of distortion was common, it is not surprising that the reaction to it, the "original innocence" doctrine, was basically not so much an Adult conclusion based on observation of children as a rejection of the op-pressive Parent and of the script dictated by it. So the al-ternative was very much a "Child" creation, a fantasy world of happiness which had to be defended against the

Parent—the wicked witches and ogres who would put spells on the Child, tie him up, and imprison him.

Yet we can learn from both kinds of mistake, and also from the truths that both were groping for. We can see that, in one way, those who want only to set the Child free from grown-up influence were, and are, right. We can confirm this doctrine by observation of children. And equally we can observe the fact that children inherit evil—in the influence of others and in their own need for self-understanding, reassurance, and acceptance, which makes them vulnerable to those influences. We can see the story of the Fall of Man from innocence to sin in this true tale in Leila Berg's story about a little boy and a little girl who played together every day. Johnny's mother went to work, and Mandy's did not, so Johnny had his meals at Mandy's home and went home at night; they were never apart if they could help it. When they were five they went off together for their first day at school.

Mandy came home—without Johnny.

"Where's Johnny, then?" said her mother.

A haughty shrug. Silence.

"Where is he?"

Silence.

"Is he coming later?"

Silence. . . .

"Isn't he having tea today?"

Silence.

"What's the matter? Where's Johnny? Have you had a quarrel? What's happened?"

"Well," said Mandy, tossing her head with what Blake called experience, "he never told me he was black!"

So, with the tones of voice, the raised eyebrows, the whispers and rewards, the sniggers and kisses and slaps, the world stains the child with "original sin" from birth and even before, and it is *his* sin, not an "external application" to be erased by right teaching, but a part of his very mind, his deepest self. Once we realize this, we see how right, too, the insistence of Christians has been on the need to teach children goodness, to counteract sin. Nowadays we do not like to think of children as sinful. That is sheer sentimentality and defeatism. Children are human, and humans are evil, yet capable of the very life of God. We are rightly appalled by the things done to children in the name of religion, yet irreligion can be as brutal, for in both cases it is not religion that is at issue, but simply the Parent desire to eradicate opposition. "You're not O.K. unless I say so," which means "unless you agree with me." We are suspicious of the invocation of the Old Testament God of wrath, who says "thou shalt not," but he is a creation not of the Hebrew religious spirit but of a selective exegesis made by that Communal Parent of Jews and Christians needing to assert authority and elaborating rules to avoid argument. It ignores the equally Old Testament God who comes as Bridegroom or loving Father, who comforts and reassures the frightened Child, and then strengthens the bewildered Adult, explaining, demonstrating, encouraging to fresh efforts, pointing out the way of integrity and maturity, the fullness of life. Here is the voice of the Servant of Yahweh, symbol of Israel itself, and also of the Savior, as the "second Isaiah" expresses it:

> He said to me, "You are my servant (Israel)
> in whom I shall be glorified";
> while I was thinking, "I have toiled in vain,
> I have exhausted myself for nothing";
>
> and all the while my cause was with Yahweh,
> my reward with my God.
> I was honored in the eyes of Yahweh,
> my God was my strength. [Isaiah 49:3-5]

This is the voice of the Child, happy to discover that his Parent is not condemning and restricting him but actually showing him how to grow up—become Adult. In a later passage, the prophet speaks as God's messenger, giving an account of what God told him to do, and we must remember that this is Jewish and Christian Scripture— "Holy Writ," that is, these are sayings repeated and repeated so as to become the Communal Parent, passed on to every generation by the individual Parent—whether it be mother or father, minister or rabbi:

> The spirit of the Lord Yahweh has been given to me,
> for Yahweh has anointed me.
> He has sent me to bring good news to the poor,
> to bind up hearts that are broken;
>
> to proclaim liberty to captives,
> freedom to those in prison;
> to proclaim a year of favor from Yahweh,
> a day of vengeance for our God,
>
> to comfort all those who mourn and to give them
> for ashes a garland;
> for mourning robe the oil of gladness,
> for despondency, praise.
> They are to be called "terebinths of integrity,"
> planted by Yahweh to glorify him.
>
> They will rebuild the ancient ruins,
> they will raise what has long lain waste,
> they will restore to the ruined cities,
> all that has lain waste for ages past. [Isaiah 61:1–4]

The first part of this passage is a hymn of the rejoicing Child, assured of his goodness and set free. The "shades of the prison house" are removed. Instead, there is celebration, an ecstasy of joy because God loves. A little girl of seven once rushed up to her mother, exclaiming "Mummy, don't you sometimes feel so glad of God that you want to rush about and shout and hug people?" The "vengeance" is a vengeance on the enemies of the Child, those who humiliate and despise him. They are gone, they simply have

no power any more! No wonder one girl of nine, realizing
what this meant, was so moved that she had to hide, at
moments, to cry with emotion, because "God is so good."

But after the rejoicing comes the work. There is something that has to be done, not by God but by the liberated
human being. The Adult must take over, must be strong
and sturdy, like a well-planted tree. Aware of his value,
sure that God loves him, even the small child can begin to
take hold of a task, the mending and rebuilding of the
broken City of Man. This is a tremendous discovery—God
loves me, God wants me, God has work for me to do. The
Adult in the child is able to be adventurous, confident that
he is trusted and can cope, even though he may make
mistakes. He is God's "terebinth of integrity."

It is worth remarking that part of this passage was used
by Jesus as the "text" to explain to people in the syna-
gogue at Nazareth what he knew his own mission to be.
He was the one sent to "proclaim liberty to captives," and
the captive is the human being, shut in by all those prejudices, fears, and hates that the Parent instills into the infant mind from the beginning. It has been the frequent
mistake of the "age of innocence" school of thought to
suppose that, since the Parent has corrupted and tortured
the minds of children, therefore there must be *no* Parent,
only the unfettered Child. But, as we have seen, the
unguided Child becomes bewildered and despairing, and
eventually rebellious. If he gets no deliberate Parent guidance, he will look for it and find it—in books, pop groups,
dreams, or anyone who seems to know what life is all
about.

One of the boys in William Golding's *Lord of the Flies*
says this at the point in the story when their shipwrecked,
adultless group is beginning to lose its grip on order, hier-
archy, and a sense of priorities:

> "We're all drifting and things are going rotten. At
> home there was always a grownup. Please, sir; please,
> miss, and then you got an answer. How I wish!"

"I wish my auntie was here."

"I wish my father. Oh, what's the use?"

"Keep the fire going." [This is the signal-fire, to tell any passing ship of their plight, which the other boys are neglecting]. . . .

"Grownups know things," said Piggy. "They ain't afraid of the dark. They'd meet and have tea and discuss. Then things 'ud be all right—". . . .

"They wouldn't quarrel—"

"Or break my specs—"

"Or talk about a beast—"

However restrictive and wrong, by Adult standards, the Parent may be—it is needed. The seeking, hopeful Child needs a Parent, and he knows in some odd way that the human Parent, the voice of mother, father, or teacher, should somehow have a deeper source. Eve Lewis, the child-psychologist mentioned earlier, noticed, as many others have done, the way in which children devise rituals of worship and propitiation, even when there is nothing in their religious background that could have suggested it to them. She tells how

I once watched a group of boys, all of whom seemed to be about the age of eleven, light a fire. When it was going well they passed their hands and feet several times through the flames. Then they lit pieces of wood from the fire and held them up like torches, while they walked round the flames, intoning a kind of chant—there were no words—and bowing deeply to the fire. . . . I was reminded of the new fire and of Easter, and of some kind of purification rite.

These children were aware of sin, at a much deeper level than the sense of guilt inculcated by the Parent about individual actions such as stealing or lying. They felt a need for purification, a need to be free of something which

was not the "real self" so that they might discover a communion with whatever was symbolized by the hot, aspiring flames. Probably there was nothing in their ordinary
lives to show them how this could really happen, but the
Child in them knew it, and acted it out, trying to bring it to
the attention of the Adult, so that something could be
done. In practice, however, it takes the Parent to explain
how this can "really be true." Without the guiding Parent,
the Child cannot interpret such need in a positive way.
Usually, Parent rituals and rules make a framework of living, which is reassuring, even if it leaves the big questions
and needs, implied by such a Child ritual, unsatisfied. But
the need is very strong and fundamental. In the absence of
a "religious" type of Parent guidance, this need can surface in violent, terrifying forms. The "not O.K." Child
seeks to propitiate or conquer the mysterious powers
within him, guided only be his own fears, which find a
concrete ritual form when they are shared. In *The Lord of
the Flies*, the boys on the desert island have half-believed
fantasies about a mysterious "beast" in the forest, which
they think they have seen, but are not sure. (It is, in fact,
the body of a dead parachutist, moved around by the wind
in his still-attached parachute.) In a half-mock ritual, some
of them try to "exorcise" this fear with aggressive chants
and dances, but in the end their own ritual seizes them
and controls them. "Kill the beast! Cut his throat! Spill his
blood!" they chant. And when another boy crawls into the
crazed, yelling circle, they identify him with the "beast"
and, in a frenzy of fear and hate, kill him. The Child alone
is as easily a murderer as a mystic. As Piggy said, "Grown-
ups know things," and the right Parent interprets and supports the mystic "instinct" of the Child. But it has to be
the right Parent—not the one that has itself been warped
by Child-fears hardened in next generation Parent con-
demnations and superstitions. For this to happen, the vil-
lainous ogre-Parent has to be banished by the consoling,
liberating, fairy-godmother Parent. And this is the true task

of the religious tradition, the Communal Parent, repeating inherited wisdom and making it available. The Gospel message is this kind of fairy-godmother, undoing the evil spell, clothing the outcast in finery, "for ashes a garland," just like Cinderella.

We know, sadly and bitterly, that the very message of freedom has been twisted in order to imprison, but that is no reason to refuse the real message to the children who need it. "Unless you become as little children, you cannot enter the Kingdom of Heaven." Perhaps this is partly because the Child in little children is still receptive, willing to believe the message of freedom, unsuspicious and open. "Of such is the Kingdom of Heaven," not because they are without sin—we have seen how sin is the human condition re-created inexorably in each generation by the fears and hates of the one before—but because when God tells them "You're O.K.," they believe it, and are willing to be set free.

The work of the human parents and teachers in religious formation, then, is to pass on the message as clearly as possible, in word and in act. In their voices should sound the voice of the Communal Parent, the Christian community as God's messenger, "telling it like it is," in the uncompromising way that the catch-phrase implies, without letting their own private Parent get in the way. It cannot be done absolutely. Even the best mother and father and minister and teacher will find that other, unliberated Parent edging in. But then, it is quite possible to tell the child this, so that his Adult can learn to discriminate. "That's just my mom feeling mean because she's had a bad day, that's not what God really thinks," the astute Adult in the small child will reflect, when Mother has raged that "God doesn't like little boys who tell lies," or hit their sisters or talk back to important grown-ups. He will know this because that same mother, in a calmer moment, has explained the difference. "Sometimes when I'm worried I say things I don't mean—just like you. I know it's not true, even when I'm saying it. I'll try not to, though." Even a three-year-old can get that one sorted out without much trouble.

This applies especially in the difficult area of "morality." It is scarcely necessary, nowadays, to stress the need to avoid making God into a kind of supercop, watching and waiting, with an armory of fearsome punishments for the offender. Yet there is a sense in which the "God of wrath" is a necessary and reassuring symbol of the liberating God. For the child can see, all around him, the consequence of sin, and it is bad. The child with a drunken father or a sadistic teacher, the child whose family is made homeless or whose brother goes to jail, will not be reassured simply by being told "God is good—he doesn't want bad things to happen." That just makes God look like a well-meaning old muddler, certainly no help in coping with real life. It is better to realize that when people do wrong, evil consequences follow, God has told us this, so that we know how things are. When people shut out God, they shut themselves in with their own badness, they refuse to be set free. So they are still in prison. This is something the emerging Adult can verify, by observation, with the right "Parent" guidance and reassurance. It is a bitter knowledge, but necessary and healthy. The boys on William Golding's island were choir-boys, presumably reared on a Parent-diet of religious statements, if only during church services. But they did not know about evil; morality for them was doing what they were told by grown-ups. When evil made itself felt among them, even those who obscurely recognized it could not face it, they had to pretend it was, as Piggy asserted, "an accident." But evil is not an accident. That is why, for all the terrible mistakes of a one-sided doctrine, those Christian educators who assumed that children were prone to evil and in need of constant guidance and correction were less wrong in practice than those who wanted to leave the heaven-born Child soul untouched by human hands, like factory-wrapped food. But it

is touched by the hands of human folly and misery as soon
as it enters the world. Hence the huge responsibility of
religious teachers of the young, and the great need for a
strong, vital tradition, the Communal Parent, whose words
can be and must be tested by the Adult, but which has the
job of setting the Adult free to do so.

Grown-ups can even pass on the right message when
they themselves do not realize the need of the Child and
when their own religious notions are limited and Parent-
oriented. Provided they let the Communal Parent come
through, the Gospel message can still be heard. An example of this occurs in the well-loved children's classic
Heidi, when the mountain-bred child, lonely and homesick
in the city, is unable to talk about it with the well-meaning
but stuffy and narrow-minded people among whom she
lives. Even the kind Grandmother of the family does not
understand what is making Heidi unhappy and can only
tell her to "pray to God" for help. Heidi prays, and nothing happens, so (her Adult drawing its own conclusions)
she stops praying. Parent-religion is a failure. But meanwhile Heidi learns to read, and as a reward is given an il-
lustrated book, evidently of New Testament parables,
which she loves because of one particular picture. It
shows the Prodigal Son at home before he leaves on his
travels, a young man on a mountain side, among sheep and
goats. This picture reminds Heidi of her beloved moun-
tain-home. Reading the story, she does not notice the message about sin and repentance. To her it is a story of exile
and homecoming (a perfectly valid interpretation of the
Gospel symbolism). So the book of the parables of Jesus
does what the grown-ups could not do—it passes on the
real Gospel message of freedom and love: "When she read
the tales aloud the scenes seemed to grow more beautiful
and distinct, and then grandmother would explain and tell
her more about them." (Here we can see the proper interaction of individual Parent and Communal Parent, in
the same person perhaps, and indistinguishable to the

Child, but nevertheless importantly distinct, for the one
fulfills and corrects and explains the other.)

> Still the picture she liked best was the one of the
> shepherd leaning on his staff with his flock around
> him in the midst of the green pasture, for he was at
> home and happy. . . . Then came the picture where
> he was seen far from his father's house, obliged to
> look after swine, and he had grown pale and thin from
> the husks which were all he had to eat. Even the sun
> seemed here less bright and everything looked gray
> and misty. But there was a third picture . . . . the old
> father with outstretched arms running to meet and em-
> brace his returning and repentant son. . . . That was
> Heidi's favorite tale, which she read over and over
> again, aloud and to herself, and she was never tired of
> hearing the grandmother explain it to her and Clara.

To Heidi, the story is first of all a personal promise that
she will go home to her grandfather in the mountains. But
the explanations add another dimension, for she realizes, if
only dimly, that it is God who liberates, who leads the
wanderer home and welcomes him. The two levels of symbolism complement each other. So, later, she is helped to
leave behind her first notion of God, as a powerful Person
who could answer her prayer but did not, for obscure reason of his own, and to come instead to a deeper understanding, of a God who is still the loving, welcoming Father, even if prayers remain "unanswered." God, she
realizes, is not a distant, impersonal Governor, but someone to know and love, someone who makes you grow up.
A new and more subtle understanding by the Adult con-
firms the relief of the comforted Child.

One of the things upon which the Christian Communal
Parent has insisted throughout its history is ritual and celebration. Some sects, it is true, have seen that this can easily be purely a Parent proceeding, imposed on the Child to

keep it quiet. They have abandoned ritual in worship (though it usually reasserts itself in home celebrations, or secular ones, like one English Quaker who has a great enthusiasm for the celebration of royal occasions). But though, naturally, it is the Parent who decides the time, place, and form of ritual worship and celebration, the real "celebrant" is the Child. Genuine ritual is an expression of Child needs, hopes, and aspirations, at a preverbal as well as verbal level. It makes possible that essential "meeting" of Child and Adult, where the Child says, "I want! I want!—I don't know what I want!" And the Adult replies, *"This* is what you want—God." And by bringing these together—the inchoate mystical longing of the Child and the careful reflection and decision of the Adult—real religious practice begins to create the wholeness of the son of God. The inner urge to adore, to search, to give, is linked to the Adult understanding of the Gospel message which says, "This is real, you can be free, God is within you, he prays in you." And it is the Communal Parent that makes this possible.

A book called *An Episode of Sparrows* by Rumer Godden tells the story of a little girl abandoned by her mother (a vaudeville actress), who lives with her mother's former landlord, a kind and idealistic man. However, he loses his money and cannot care for her any more. Lovejoy, as the child is called, has a great deal of self-respect and enterprise and has always taken care of herself and her clothes. With great difficulty, during the months her mother has failed to turn up, she has also made herself a tiny garden in a patch of waste ground behind a church. But the church is to be rebuilt, the beloved square of growing things is to be bulldozed away, and Lovejoy is to go to a "home" run by nuns. However, before that, Lovejoy has made the acquaintance of religion in the form of a gaudy Madonna in the church. All she knows is, as a boy called Tip tells her, "You can ask Her for things." But, in a rage when she hears about the destruction of her garden, she throws a stone and breaks the statue. The worst happens: her liberty and her little garden (the one is a symbol of the other) are both taken away, and there is a scene in the home in which Angela, a busy "do-gooder," who takes her there, represents perfectly the wrong kind of religious Parent. But there is another person who knows what is really needed. " 'Lovejoy, do you know why this house is called the House of Compassion?' asked Angela. . . ."

"Compassion is pity," Angela told Lovejoy now. "This home is called that because it's a home for children who are to be pitied." The Sister made a quick movement and Angela said, "I'm afraid, Sister, this sometimes needs to be said. Lovejoy is far too opinionated. Do you know why they are to be pitied?" she asked Lovejoy.

"No," said Lovejoy.

"Because they are destitute, which means they have nothing. Nothing at all," said Angela, "except what some kind person chooses to give them. You should be grateful and not criticize," said Angela.

"But I can think?" said Lovejoy. She meant it as a question but it sounded bald and rude.

"You had better think," said Angela with an edge on her voice. "Think. If there were no kind people, what would you do?"

"I'd—" Lovejoy's face was far more expressive than Angela had thought. She looked, not masked, shut in, but eager and happy, like another child. . . . Then her eyes came back to Angela and the eagerness died.

"You see," said Angela.

"Yes. I have to have kind people," said Lovejoy.

So far, the image of religion, of the very love of a God of Compassion, is of the Parent who will protect the Child—but only in return for unconditional surrender of the Adult to the Parent. And that kills the "O.K. Child," there is

nothing left but the abject, frightened beggar, the Child
who knows "even God thinks I'm not O.K." and can only
hope for little bits of comfort—on conditions—from the
grown-ups who claim to know God's opinions and wishes.
But that is not all. Lovejoy is taken to see the rest of the
home, including the chapel, and the Sister tells her, "If
ever you find things difficult and don't feel very happy,
you can come in here." And there is a statue—just like the
one she broke.

She [the Sister] had expected Lovejoy would find
the chapel strange, even bewildering, but Lovejoy
walked past her as if it were familiar, then stood as if
she had been struck still. "He*llo!*" It was a greeting,
not an exclamation. On her papers had been written
Sunday school, church, nil, but she slid into a pew
and knelt down.

After a moment Sister Agnes came and sat beside
her.

"She was in a church I knew," whispered Lovejoy.

"The statue?" Lovejoy nodded, her breath held. . . .

Then Sister Agnes distinctly heard her whisper, "Hail
Mary."

"We don't teach you to pray to Mary," said the Sister gently.

Lovejoy did not know the difference between Angli-
can and Roman Catholic; even she had not fathomed
all the vagaries of grown-ups; she had wondered why
there were no candles, she missed their warmth and
the live sounds of the clicking of beads—she understood beads now—the pattering of prayers.

Tip taught me and I'll do what Tip taught me forever and ever, said Lovejoy silently.

"And we don't cross ourselves."

I do, said Lovejoy silently.

"You can honour her as the mother of Our Lord but
you must not give her supernatural powers."

Supernatural powers, supernatural babies, and lions
with wings. A wave of such homesickness came over
Lovejoy for the Street, the church, the garden, Jiminy
Cricket, that she could not speak. . . .

She shut her eyes. She had meant to bring Jiminy
Cricket but—I broke the statue to bits, thought Lovejoy, and I couldn't go back into the church. It's queer,
she thought, when you're kind to people you can
forget them but when you're not, you can't. When she
had stolen the candle money the statue had been
hooded up in purple but this was evidently worse,
because all these days Lovejoy had felt that it was she,
Lovejoy, who was swathed. "I didn't mean it," she
said, still hearing the crash. "If I didn't mean it, then
it shouldn't count," she argued, but it counted and she
had felt muffled, hidden in sorrow and grief, and now
the statue was here again, with the sky-blue robe,
white veil, pink hands and face, lilies, and gilt plate
on the back of her head.

"No supernatural powers," said Sister Agnes firmly.
Lovejoy dropped her lids.

A nun came to the chapel door, and Sister Agnes got
up. "Wait here a moment," she said.

Outside a bell clanged, and presently Lovejoy heard
a sound like school, the sound of children's feet
marching. She leaned her head against the pew rail
and shut her eyes. Even her sharp little brain could
see no way out of it. She had to have kind people.

The feet were coming nearer, the din of voices; then
there was a clap of hands and complete obedient silence.

Steps came towards the chapel—to fetch me,
thought Lovejoy in a panic. In a moment someone
would say, "Come along."

All the things said to children rose in her mind. "Do
as you're told." "Don't answer back." "Come along."
"Be quiet." Lovejoy ground her teeth. Quiet, obe-

dient, grateful. All the detestable things children
should be, and all the lovely free things, thought
Lovejoy, that they must not, opinionated, cocky—she
hadn't Angela's word "cocksure." Cocky, thought
Lovejoy longingly.

The door opened. "Come along," said Sister Agnes,
but Lovejoy was praying.

"Hail Mary," prayed Lovejoy between her teeth,
"Mary, make me cocky and independent."

Lovejoy's prayer is the right prayer, and she went to the
right source for an answer. Her symbol of the freedom of
the Gospel of Jesus was a gaudy, mass-produced plaster
statue of his Mother, but Lovejoy's human instinct was
right. And somehow, through all the centuries of distortion
and failure, the Communal Parent of the Christian tradition has managed to hand on that message intact (though
often with curious accretions), ready to be picked up by
anyone tuned in, like Lovejoy, and not switched off by fear
and suspicion. Above all, it can be picked up by children,
whose innocence is still beating strongly and not yet extin-
guished by the frightened Parent of a world that does not
believe in the possibility of freedom. This radical innocence is there, at the very heart of that real and terrible
sin that is our condition, our world. "Mary, make me cocky
and independent." How else can the children grow up to
"rebuild the ancient ruins" of a world destroyed by its
own age-old sin?

Lovejoy is a "story" child, but not long ago, one real-life
little girl died of a painful illness at the age of eleven—
about the same age at which Lovejoy prayed to be "cocky
and independent." Anne had had a very different life, protected and carefully brought up by a mother whose own
faith was one deepened by the loss of her adored husband
when her children were still quite small. But Anne was
like Lovejoy in one respect—to her, God did not mean
conformity, restriction, and reward-for-being-good. He

meant joy and freedom, freedom to be herself. He also
meant discipline and effort, but effort for the sake of love
is joy, even when it is painful. And Anne knew that she
wanted to see, to see the All that, very early, she had
glimpsed behind the thick curtains of religious words and
actions. "I want to *see* Him," she told her mother once, but
this upset the poor woman so that her child did not say it
again. She still thought it, though. The Child in Anne had
learned, "God thinks you're O.K.," for the Parent told her
this, in the voice of her mother and of her teachers. (She
was lucky to have very good, sensitive ones.) So her Adult
reason, as it reflected on life and people, concluded that
the greatest thing of all must be to see, and truly know,
that God which both the Child's inchoate desires and the
comforting Parent voice told her was desirable above all
things. Anne, "cocky and independent," stuck to this opin-
ion and refused to be distracted by the interesting alternatives around her or frightened by the pain and helplessness of a long illness. Perhaps, after all, those who believe
in the essential God-relatedness of the Child are right, for
at the end, the Parent could no longer comfort, and the
Adult had nothing to contribute. It had done its work. But
the Child, no longer afraid or cowed, but "cocky and independent," assured and confident, began to see. All the
human race cries "Lord, that I may see!" Anne, the day
before she died, called in great excitement to her little
brother and sister, "Come and see! Oh—look how beautiful it is!" They saw nothing, and she could not explain.

2

"Like Little Children"

"I FELT that my confirmation was one of the most solemn and important events and acts in my life," wrote the young Princess Victoria, heiress to the throne of England but still muffled in the folds of feminine watchfulness every moment of day and night.

I trusted that it might have a salutary effect on my mind. I felt deeply repentant for all that I had done which was wrong and trusted in God Almighty to strengthen my heart and mind, and to forsake all that is bad and follow all that is virtuous and right. I went with a firm determination to become a good Christian, to try and comfort my dear Mamma in all her griefs, trials and anxieties, and to become a dutiful and affectionate daughter to her. Also to be obedient to my *dear* Lehzen, who has done so much for me. I was dressed in a white lace dress, with a white crepe bonnet with a wreath of white roses round it. I went in a chariot with my dear Mamma. . . ."

And in a chariot with "dear Mamma" Victoria remained, spiritually as well as physically for some time. Confirmation has become the official, recognized "moment of decision" for many traditional Christians, the time for the conscious acceptance of adult responsibility—yet often, as in Victoria's case, it is clearly a decision to conform to the Parent dictates, rather than the definitive assumption by the Adult of responsibility for Christian decision. If Victoria did have that kind of moment, it was probably that of her accession to the throne, when she realized—in a moment of revelation for which all the years of expectation of royal dignity had not prepared her—that she was her own mistress. Her first expressed wish as Queen was "to be by myself for an hour," and her first royal command was that her bed should be moved out of her mother's room. Victoria's real spiritual "coming of age" was not marked by a religious ceremony but by an assertion of independence of her mother. Her "conversion" was from subject to queen, and in a sense that is what it always is. "You are royal priesthood, a consecrated nation", St. Paul told his rabble of converted laborers, small tradesmen, and slaves.

> The Spirit you received is not the spirit of slaves bringing fear into your lives again; it is the spirit of sons, and it makes us cry out "Abba!, Father!" The Spirit himself and our spirit bear united witness that we are children of God. And if we are children we are heirs as well: heirs of God and coheirs with Christ, sharing his suffering so as to share his glory. [Rom. 8:14–17]

If the conclusions of the previous chapter are valid, the Gospel message invites the Child to shed all the fears and restraints that have imprisoned him, and to recognize that it possesses "the glorious liberty of the sons of God." This means casting off the hold of the Parent, as Governor, and this emancipation brings with it a huge sense of release,

joy, and hope. This is the experience of "conversion" and,
typically, it is an overwhelming one.

One of the most famous conversions was that of Blaise
Pascal. Both his parents were from respectable professional families, and his father was a highly intelligent man.
His mother had died when he was three. After her death,
the elder sister, Gilberte, took charge of the household,
but it was Etienne, his father, who decided to be "mother,
father, and tutor," as one biographer puts it, to his children. Etienne was a brilliant educator, a man with a deep
interest in language and science and the ability to inspire
that interest in a child. A strong bond of family affection
made learning pleasant, and, wrote Gilberte later, Blaise
"wanted to know the reasons for everything . . . always
and in everything the truth was the one goal of his mind.
. . ." This education was almost exclusively intellectual,
for although affectionate the family was undemonstrative.
Perhaps the loss of his wife made Etienne wary of forming
another deep attachment. Blaise evidently admired his father, and as his father's greatest ambition was that his son
should shine in the mathematical sciences, shine he did.
When, later, Etienne took on the necessary but exacting
job of tax assessor, Blaise watched his father endlessly por-
ing over the columns of figures, and proceeded to invent a
calculating machine. It was compact and efficient, the forerunner of the computer.

But this education left out a lot. It left out history, and
"language" meant only grammar and syntax, not literature.
Religion was limited to the simple teaching regarded as
suitable for a child—but hardly for *that* child. No doubt
his father expected his son to fill the gaps himself, and
concentrated on the things he himself was good at, but the
effect was that Blaise's "Parent" commanded that life
should be dealt with in strictly logical and philosophical
form. His writings contain no evidence of sensitivity to
natural beauty, and *"poête mais non honnête homme"* was
one of his later aphorisms, meaning not so much that poets

are liars as that a poet lacks something—there is a weakness that prevents him being completely "man." That was the view impressed on his Parent, certainly.

But Blaise Pascal, admired and successful as a philosopher and a scientific genius, became restless, gloomy, and "empty," as he put it. To fill the void he entered into a frenzied social whirl. He hunted, danced, and—typically—planned to write a study which would "reduce to an exact art, with the vigor of mathematical demonstration, the incertitude of chance, thus creating a new science which could justly claim the stupefying title, the geometry of hazard!" Also, he could find no faith in the God whom he knew only in childish terms, or as a philosophical abstraction that left him cold and afraid. He became more and more disgusted with a world that could not satisfy him. The celebrated, fêted Pascal was in despair. So he went to visit his younger sister, Jaqueline, who was a nun, and told her how he felt. He was reaching back to the Child in himself, whose experiences Jaqueline had, to a great extent, shared. Besides, she had a serene faith, and he had none. She wrote to Gilberte about him:

> In the midst of all his great occupations, and among all those things which might have combined to attach him to the world—he had been longing to get away from all that . . . he had now broken away from everybody as never before. . . . And yet, he felt completely abandoned by God. . . . But he believed that he was merely making an intellectual struggle to find God; it was not a genuine movement of himself towards God. [Ernest Mortimer, *Blaise Pascal*]

He was right. His Adult self was aware of the fact that the only way his Parent allowed him to look for God was unsatisfactory—useless, in fact. But he was helpless, for that was the only way he knew. Others, in his situation, have given up and become atheists or cynics. But he did

not give up. Instead, still seeing no way ahead, in his need
he went on visiting Jaqueline. Perhaps she reasserted in
his mind the influence of the other Parent voice, that of his
dead mother, comforting and reassuring, telling him that to
be open, to give onself, is not suicide, but hope. Certainly
Jaqueline felt that he was "like a child," and she his
mother-in-God.

Two months after those visits began, the moment came
that, afterwards, he recorded hastily on a scrap of paper
before the first impressions could fade. Later he copied it
out on parchment, and after his death both these records
were found sewn into the lining of his waistcoat. The
parchment has been lost, but the original scribbled paper
still exists, the record of a moment "out of time" that
lasted in fact about two hours and in which he "saw," in
an experience too whole and intense ever to be completely described. It changed his whole life, releasing in
him all the greatness of heart, intensity of love, enthusiasm
and even fun that had been suppressed. He did not lose or
despise his terrific intellectual gifts, but they were transformed by a new freedom and "suppleness." The famous
"memorial," too long to give in full, shows no more than
the "skeleton" of his experience of conversion, but it
shows clearly enough the nature of the transformation:

> From about half-past ten in the evening until about
> half-past twelve
>
> ### FIRE
>
> God of Abraham, God of Isaac, God of Jacob, not of
>   the philosophers and savants.
>   Certitude. Certitude, Feeling and Joy. Peace
>   God of Jesus Christ.
>   My God and thy God.
>   "Thy God shall be my God"
> Forgetfulness of the world and of everything
>   except God

He is to be found in the ways taught by the
  Gospel.
      Grandeur of the human soul.
Righteous Father, the world hath not known thee, but
  I have known thee.
    Joy, joy, joy, tears of joy. . . . [ibid.]

We remember the little boys, cleansing their hands in
the newly lit fire and then lifting the fire in worship. Fire
cleanses and liberates. Children are fascinated by fire,
whereas grown-ups tend to fear it or just use it. The
dreaming, aspiring Child is released, to adore and to love,
he does not depend on the "philosophers and wise men,"
the Parents, however well-informed and prudent. It is interesting that Pascal quotes the words of Ruth, the foreign
woman, who promised to go with her widowed mother-in-
law, the Hebrew Naomi, forsaking her own people. Ruth's
Parent said "You belong to us," Ruth's Adult said, "I love
my husband's people, and I will go with Naomi—thy people shall be my people, and thy God shall be my God."
That was Ruth's conversion, and in it the Child found fulfillment and joy in the love of Naomi and Naomi's God.
Pascal, in also leaving his Parent, was enabled to do so by
faith. It was that "leap in the dark," typical of real conversion, when reason and common sense came to be—not denied but transcended, for only the Child has enough trust
to surrender into what appears to the Adult to be "nothing" and to the Parent a threat, a danger (which it is). Yet,
the Child's emancipation is also the Adult's emancipation,
for the "O.K. Child" has the self-confidence to make
proper use of the Adult, and to set about the work of the
whole human person.
So Elizabeth Fry found. Her Parent, though no intellectual giant, was an advocate of beauty, order, elegance, and
family affection. High principle, moderation, the "golden
mean" so beloved of the "enlightened" philosophy of the
time—all these were young Betsy Gurney's Parent. Her

family were Quakers, but "gay" Quakers who despised the
strictness of the "plain" Quakers. Like young Victoria, she
thought she could "be good" according to a plan, sensible,
high-minded but not "enthusiastic." "Enthusiasm" meant
unstable, excitable religion. Not at all the proper thing!
And to the "gay Gurneys" the "plain" Quakers with their
sober dress and manner and oddities of speech were the
very symbol of "enthusiasm" and the pitfalls of religion
run mad.

"I am seventeen today," she wrote in her journal of
May, 1787. "Am I a happier or a better creature than I was
this time twelve months? I know I am happier; I think I
am better, I hope I shall be much better this day year than
I am now. I hope to be quite an altered person, to have
more knowledge, to have my mind in greater order; and
my heart, too, that wants to be put in order as much, if not
more, than any part of me, it is in such a fly away state."

So much for good, solid Parent plans. But there were
nightly dreams—dreams of darkness, death, of the sea roll-
ing over her, as it had done when a woman at the seaside
had ducked her under the cold waves. Night after night
she dreamed that the dark sea swept over her and
drowned her, and woke sweating with fear. Her mother's
death left her without a comforting refuge. She felt de-
fenseless, and, like Pascal, "empty." She struggled to have
"a good mind," to "avoid idleness and dissipation." She
felt "lower and lower in my own estimation," yet she also
felt an obscure sense that she was capable of something
different. She thought that religion would help, would
"make her good," but "I don't feel any real religion; I
should think those feelings impossible to obtain, for even
if I thought all the Bible was true, I do not think I could
make myself feel it." Anyway, she was not sure it *was* true.
How could one be sure of God? "I have no real faith in
any sort of religion." Also, "I have the greatest fear of
religion, because I never saw a person religious who was
not enthusiastic." To be uncontrolled, wild, inelegant,

crude, that was *the* crime, said her Parent. To be a *Quaker* (that is, a "plain" Quaker)—Never! It was against all the family tradition, the strongest Parent commands.

Whatever her plans, her eighteenth year did in fact see her "quite altered," but not as she hoped. When she went to the Quaker Meeting on February 4th of 1798, she was mildly curious, because an American Friend was to be there and he might speak. That would be a pleasant change from the usual boredom. All the Gurney girls hated the hours at the Meeting House in Goat's Lane. "Being Goatified," they called it. All of them, Betsy not least, loved pretty clothes, and some stricter Friends disapproved when they came to Meeting wearing red cloaks and ribbons. Then William Savery was "led" to speak, and Betsy found herself listening. Afterwards, they all went back to Uncle Joseph Gurney's house, where they had dinner with the visitor. William Savery had been shocked by the worldly clothes of the "gay Gurneys," but he was a courteous man, and he did not refuse their company or express his feelings. There was another Meeting that evening, and her uncle, realizing that some inner upheaval was taking place in Betsy, thought he might help her, and arranged for her to travel to the Meeting alone with the visitor.

Betsy's conversion was not the lightning kind. Her entry in her journal next day was extremely cautious, weighing up her Parent opinions against the desires of her "feeling" Child, newly conscious of the latent power available to the liberated, "saved" (O.K.) person.

Today much has passed of a very serious nature. I have had a faint light spread over my mind . . . it has caused me to feel a *little* religion. My imagination has been worked upon and I fear all that I have felt will go off. I fear it now, though at first I was frightened that a plain Quaker should have made so deep an impression on my feelings, but how truly prejudiced in

me to think because good came from a Quaker I
should be led away by enthusiasm and folly!

Elizabeth's Adult is well in control, evidently, and indeed
the type of Parent-impression the Gurneys received
always emphasized the importance of careful, rational,
personal decision, which is another example of how the
right kind of Parent can actually assist the necessary liberation from the restrictive Parent. Thus, Elizabeth had permission from her Parent to examine the data of that Parent,
and judge it with her Adult. She was free even to give real
weight to *feelings*, the Child influence: "I have *felt* there
is a God. I have been devotional and my mind has been
led away from the follies that it is mostly wrapped up in."
    These "follies," like Pascal's frenetic social activities,
are the futile attempts of the unliberated Child to comfort
and distract itself. William Savery's words, on the contrary,
had been "like a refreshing shower upon parch'd up earth
that had been dried up for ages. It has not made me unhappy," she adds in some surprise, since her family
regarded religious people as inevitably gloomy and stern.
All the same, she recalls, "I had a painful night."
    Savery left next day and Elizabeth's extreme honesty
allows us to watch the progress of her struggle, which
was far from over. Meeting next Sunday was as boring as
ever.

Today I felt all my old irreligious feelings, my object
shall be to search, try to do right . . . but the state I
am in now makes it difficult to act . . . the more I
reason upon it, the more I get into a labyrinth of uncertainty, and my mind is so much inclined to both
scepticism and enthusiasm, that if I argue and doubt, I
shall be a total sceptic; if on the contrary, I give way to
my feelings, and, as it were, wait for religion, I may be
led away.

But, concludes Elizabeth, defying her Parent, "I am sure it is better to be so [religious] in an enthusiastic degree than not to be so at all, for it is a delightful enthusiasm."

Her father took her to London to distract her. She was distracted, but found she could not throw herself into gaiety as she wished. And a letter from Savery, though helpful and encouraging, brought up all the old repugnance for "plain" Quakers, and Elizabeth fell back on reason, the clear-eyed Adult.

> We are all governed by our feelings; now the reason why religion is far more likely to keep you in the path of virtue than any theoretical plan is that you feel . . . it acts as a furnace on your character . . . it purifies it; whereas principles of your own making are without kindling to make the fire hot enough to answer its purpose.

"FIRE," wrote Pascal in his Memorial, and the symbol of fire has been used over and over again by saints and mystics, as the living symbol was used by unreligious little boys to express their obscure need. Elizabeth had not felt that fire fully, only its warmth. (All the same, the terrible dreams of drowning stopped. In a last one she dreamed the sea came in but that she was beyond its reach.) Her struggle continued, but she seemed to reach no firm conclusion; indeed she could not. It is not possible for the imprisoned Child to secure his own release, for he has no arguments with which to oppose the powerful Parent, and the Adult, assessing evidence on its merits, finds the witness of the feeling Child confusing and disturbing, even frightening. Something else, some "third party," has to come in, as the therapist does in the clinical situation. This "third party" is one who speaks "with authority." Jesus liberated men and women from sickness and sin by words of authority. He spoke to the heart of them, em-

powering the Adult to resist the stifling Parent, and so
making way for the Child to hear and "come forth." The
voice that liberates has to have some affinity with the
dumb, imprisoned Child. Sometimes that voice stills the
Parent by speaking with greater and more evident knowledge and power. Sometimes the Parent itself, as in the
case of the best of Jewish tradition, has prepared the way,
though it remains for the Child to recognize with joy what
the Parent sayings really meant.

In Elizabeth's case, the former was true. Her father took
her on holiday to the West Country, and she met the
Quaker mystic Deborah Darby. The gentle, quiet "plain"
Quaker woman bypassed all the Gurney teaching, not con-
tradicting it, but simply asserting a greater power and a
higher value. From the first she made Betsy's "heart beat
much."

Deborah Darby "encouraged" Elizabeth. "You're O.K.,"
she convinced her, in effect. Deborah discerned Elizabeth's quality and realized her struggle, her being "sick of
the world" but unable to move ahead with confidence.
The sympathy, affection, and understanding made Betsy's
sensitive heart open. She was receptive. "This is one of
the happy and bright seasons of my life," she wrote, and in
this mood she went to Deborah Darby's house one evening.

> After we had spent a pleasant evening, my heart
> began to feel itself silenced before God. . . . I felt
> myself under the shadow of the wing of God, and I
> soon found the rest dropp'd into the same state. I felt
> there must be a meeting. There was: after sitting a
> time in awful silence—D. D. spoke. I only fear she
> says too much of what I am to be—a light *to the blind,*
> speech to the *dumb,* and *feet to the lame.* Can it be?
> . . . After the meeting my heart felt really light and as
> I walked home by starlight I looked up through nature
> to nature's God. Here I am now in Cousin Prissy's

little room—never to forget this day while life is in my body. I know now what the mountain is I have to climb. *I am to be a Quaker!*

From that moment, Elizabeth did not look back. She did not rush, she moved a step at a time, thoughtfully, but she knew where she was going, she was happy and she was whole. Her liberated Child was not, as her Parent had feared, a wild and unruly and destructive thing, but a power of joy, peace, and hope. Her Adult approved and set about using that power in constructive ways, and—this is typical of the experience of real conversion—with enormously enhanced physical energy.

Elizabeth's conversion was quiet and slow, attended by no ecstasies or outbursts. The type of conversion that is moving and spectacular has attracted more attention, most of it critical, for it seems a repulsive display of uncivilized behavior. Of course it is uncivilized. It is the Child—untrained and free—expressing his triumph. The violent type of conversion is likely to occur in cases where the Parent has strictly forbidden such a course. St. Paul's, perhaps the most famous of all conversions, was of this kind. A brilliant boy, he was trained from earliest childhood (as was the custom) in the most rigid and highly organized tradition of Rabbinical studies and way of life, and every movement of his mind was controlled by a prohibition of anything whatever that might prove the enemy of that tradition. That tradition was, in fact, under attack from all sides, and since Saul's (as he was then called) family lived not in the land of the Jews but in a Roman city, Tarsus, they were even more acutely aware of the dangers to the faith posed by foreign influences. Any deviation, any weakness toward those who deviated, was a crime against the Torah, the Law of life—against the God of Israel himself. Saul later reminded the Galatian converts "how enthusiastic I was for the traditions of my ancestors." So when the new sect of followers of Jesus began to be heard of, Saul was among those most bitterly opposed to them. They were traitors to the One God and to Moses; they deserved no pity.

We do not know when something began to stir under the surface. Perhaps it was the behavior of Stephen, whose death Saul witnessed. Stephen suffered patiently, calling down mercy not vengeance on his killers. Yet Stephen (judging by his uncompromising speech to the Council when he condemned them in detail out of the Scriptures) was just such a fiery and dedicated young man as Saul himself. Perhaps Saul had heard that speech, and his Adult, well trained to cope with difficult questions, though within certain Parent-defined limits, found itself frustrated, blocked by Parent "No Entry" signs, yet wanting to take the argument further.

Whatever the reasons, Saul's mind was in a turmoil, his firm beliefs fighting hard. His Child was hitting back, with feelings of anger and fear and desire for revenge, but his Parent tried to direct those feelings at the irritant, the "cause of all the trouble," this heretical sect that followed the Way of Jesus. This is a common Parent tactic. The person whose Parent tells him "never trust women," for instance, will be very disturbed by a woman he likes and whom he wants to trust. These disturbed feelings, which are his Child trying to find freedom to love, may be blamed on the woman, thus proving that the Parent is right, that women do strange things to your feelings, and this proves they should not be trusted. So Saul's disturbed feelings about the new sect caused him to feel violently opposed to *it*. He was "breathing threats to slaughter the Lord's disciples," but really it was his own imprisoned Child his Parent wanted to slaughter. He set off for Damascus to make more arrests, and on the way he was felled to the ground by a great light and power:

> . . . then he heard a voice saying. "Saul, Saul, why are you persecuting me?"
> "Who are you, Lord?" he asked, and the voice an-

swered, "I am Jesus, and you are persecuting me."
[Acts 9:4–5]

Whom was Saul persecuting? The followers of Jesus, obviously, and Jesus had said "Whatever you do to the least
of my brethren, you do to me." But there is more to it than
that. The act of violence hurts not only the one who is ill-
treated, it also strikes at the assailant, crippling his ability
to feel and to love the power of the Child. The "me"
whom Saul was persecuting were not only the members of
the new sect, but the Child in Saul himself, being beaten
by the outraged Parent for daring to stir. And the voice of
Jesus identified himself with that Child.

In one version of the story, the one Luke puts into Paul's
mouth in the account of his defense speech before King
Agrippa, this sentence is followed by the odd remark, "It
is hard for you, kicking like this against the goad," a reference to a Greek proverb meaning that useless resistance
only harms the rebellious ox. It is usually taken to mean
that Saul might as well give up resisting the power of God,
since it would only hurt him. Perhaps, but the essential
thing about conversion is that it is a liberation, not a surrender to superior force. Though it often requires a surrender, it is the arrogant Parent who surrenders, while the
Child triumphs. (The Child needs the Adult, too, but at
the time it is the Child who is important.) So, conceivably,
what that cryptic proverb meant was, "Your Child is taking
a beating, and while you remain under the control of your
Parent you'll get nothing but a beating." To which Saul
replied, in one version of the story, "What am I to do,
Lord?"

In the other two versions the question is not recorded,
but a reply to it is given, so the question is implicit. The
reply, on the first account, is simply, "Get up now and go
into the city and you'll be told what you have to do." The
account of the speech to Agrippa adds a kind of gloss, in-
dicating, as Paul himself realized later, what it was he

"had to do" and why: ". . . for I have appeared to you for
this reason: to appoint you as my servant and as witness of
this vision in which you have seen me. . . . *I shall deliver
you* from the people and *from the pagans, to whom I am
sending you to open their eyes. . . .*" [Acts 26:16–18]

Deborah Darby also told Elizabeth Gurney that she was to
be "a light to the blind"; but Saul's own eyes were
temporarily blind, as if his body were recording the overwhelming sense of the blindness in which he found himself.
Since, at a stroke, his all-wise, all-seeing Parent had been
conquered by a greater power, all that he knew through
his Parent (which had been his whole education and self-
respect, remember) was now darkness. No wonder he had
to be "led by the hand" into Damascus. He remained in
the dark, his mind in turmoil, his conscious thought-pat-
terns wrecked, his Adult demoralized, with no data to
work on except the impression of that searing light and
voice which had shattered his clean, orderly world. How
much his later reflections gave form to the experience as
he recorded it, we cannot tell. We do know the effect it
had, and undoubtedly his way of expressing it was as near
as he could get to describing the essential nature of that
happening. For three days he was blind and could not eat
or drink. Then a follower of Jesus, instructed in a dream,
came to him saying: "Brother Saul, I have been sent by
the Lord Jesus who appeared to you on your way here so
that you may recover your sight and be filled with the
Holy Spirit." And so it was. Just as Deborah Darby finally
freed Elizabeth Gurney from the struggle and doubts into
which her first "vision" had plunged her, so Ananias set
Saul free. He was baptized, he ate and drank, and within a
few days he was preaching the Gospel of Jesus with such
force and power of conviction that it seemed as though he
had always known the Lord. And in a sense, he had. In a
sense, we all have. But we have to discover what the
Quakers call the Inner Light and give it room to grow. The
proper role of the Parent, as we saw in the first chapter, is

to "prepare a way for the Lord," but more often the Parent (frequently with the best intentions) merely heaps up obstacles to his progress. The obstacles can sometimes be thrown down only by tremendous force, as in Saul's case, or in Pascal's, but once they are thrown down, and the Child has been rendered confident and joyful (I'm O.K.), then the untapped reserve of spiritual and physical energy is available and requires to be used. At this point, two things have to happen.

One is that an Adult has to be on hand to interpret what is going on. A conversion that takes place where there is a weak Adult does not last; it is geniune, but there is no way to understand properly what is going on, therefore the power and joy of the Child remains merely Childish—undirected and chaotic. This is true of many of the "revival type" conversions, where there is no follow-up, either in the reflective intelligence of the convert or in the interpretative efforts of minister or friends, to guide and explain. This ephemeral kind of conversion has helped to make solid Christians suspicious of emotional religion, not without reason. It is essential that the now "O.K." Child should be guided by an Adult who understands the meaning of what has happened and can decide what to do about it, for action is required. Elizabeth Gurney went home and tried to improve her spelling! She also began to teach local children to read and write, and later on she shook the whole moral foundation of the country's prison system. Pascal, already hyperactive under the direction of his Parent, responded by giving more time to prayer and Scripture study. He became calmer. Saul, always an enthusiast, became, in the freedom of the Spirit, a preacher and pastor of such indomitable energy and courage, gentleness and force, organizing ability and human sympathy, that he shook up not one system, one country, but the history of the world. He is still doing it by his letters, and there is often a note of glee in his accounts of how the Child (the archetypal Child, the Puer Aeternus who appears in early

Christian art as a very *young* Christ) does indeed "put down the mighty from their seats," as Luke's hymn of the expectant Mother of Jesus proclaims, and Paul echoes: *"Where are the philosophers now?* Where are any of our thinkers . . . today? Do you see now how God has shown up the foolishness of human wisdom?" (1 Cor. 1:20)

But Paul's Adult was both backing up and controlling the gleeful Child. The range and grasp of his mind was extraordinary, and with it he explained, exhorted, celebrated, working on both the new experience of life revealed by his regained feeling-Child, and also—and this is the other thing that has to happen—on the Parent recordings. Saul the pupil in the Jerusalem schools continued to use the rabbinical method and the great tradition of his people when he became Paul the Christian. The richness and coherence of his thought owed much to this great inheritance. Without it, he could not have done what he did; his Communal Parent had provided him with a language. It gave him the concepts, the attitudes, the words that he needed in order to understand and use the very experience which transcended that tradition. He realized in Christ the fulfilment, not the destruction, of the history and thought of his people.

In the same way, the converted Pascal was a changed man, but it was his keen, philosophy-trained mind that made him such a powerful opponent of those who seemed to him the enemies of true religion. The great Jansenist controversy in which he was involved has faded into history, and nobody is very interested in it now, though traces of it can still be found in modern religious attitudes. Pascal was not really a Jansenist, anyway, but he had friends who were, and he rushed to defend one of them against a conspiracy to disgrace him, mounted on pseudo-theological grounds, but really a matter of pique and politics. Pascal's liberated mind went to work in that defense. His famous *Lettres Provinciales* are not merely brilliant dialectic, they are witty, living prose, full of love and irony and a shrewd grasp of human motives. He was fighting men who were using true ideas to tell lies, religious con- cepts to carry out revenge. These were, indeed, Parent- dominated men. Pascal, set free, could use his highly en- dowed Parent and his feeling, enthusiastic Child, expres- sing and balancing the different wisdoms available from both, selecting and judging with his Adult.

The Parent of the converted person becomes precious. No longer oppressive, no longer a threat, it can contribute to the whole, but of course only if the Parent-recording contains things that really are useful and true, as judged by the Adult, now enlightened by the intuitive Child with his "clouds of glory." Betsy Gurney, after she became Eliza- beth Fry, still made use of that Gurney Parent in her that insisted on courtesy, gentleness, tact, neatness and ele- gance of person and manner. Many Friends disapproved; they thought her beautiful manners "stuck up"; they called their own lack of tact "honesty" and their lack of courtesy "simplicity." Elizabeth, thinking it over with her Adult, decided there was nothing wrong with good man- ners and sensitivity to other people's feelings. When, later, she began what was to be her great mission, her work for the women of Newgate, this Parent-instituted courtesy and self-respect actually made it possible for her to "get through" to desperate, demoralized women, among whom the jailers dared only to go in pairs. Although critical of her "suicidal" folly, they finally let Mrs. Fry into the wo- men's yard and locked the door behind her, expecting to see her clothes torn off, if no worse. But the Gurney tradi- tion was courtesy to all, and Elizabeth's Christian Adult approved. She simply spoke to those filthy, ragged, hate- filled creatures as she would have spoken to any other women. She spoke to the beaten and outraged Child in them, to the struggling, impotent Adult. She reassured the Child by her gentle voice and manner, and she spoke di- rectly to the Adult by what she said, for she spoke of the one subject on which she and they shared common

ground—their children. She picked up one of the dirty
toddlers who stood staring, and let him play with her gold
watch, her one "worldly" ornament, and she told the
women: "Friends, many of you are mothers. I too am a
mother. I am distressed for your children. Is there not
something we can do for these innocent little ones? Do
you want them to become real prisoners themselves? . . ."
"Something *we* can do"! The tact of the well-brought up
girl had become the love of the Christian woman.

But suppose the Parent of the converted has nothing to
contribute, as judged by the Adult, or if the Adult is too
weak to resist the vengeful Parent? In that appalling and
fascinating book *The Children of Sanchez,* Oscar Lewis
records meticulously the accounts given by a father and
four grown children of their life in the slums of Mexico
City. Early sex, corrupted religion, hunger, madness, despair—these were the experiences of the Child in all of
them, and the Parent record consists of blows, contradictory orders, outbursts of rage, and equally irrational outbursts of tearful affection. Such treatment produced differing results in each, according to their temperament and
their sex and the way their parents thought of them. The
elder girl in the family, Consuelo, grew up with a morbid
fear of sex and a hatred of all males because of the way her
father and older brother treated her, and the talk of the
other women. She struggled to get an education; she
learned shorthand, she wanted something, something different. Eventually she married just to get away from home.
Her young husband loved her, but sex was such a horror to
her that she could not even pretend. Her "not O.K." Child
could not be reassured, she fought and wept and hated,
and prayed to die, prayed to the God who was a symbol of
escape, of self-respect, of beauty. She became pregnant
and miscarried after a fall. This was the ultimate shame in
a culture that measures a woman by her fertility, and a humiliation to her husband; yet he still loved her. She was
ill, mentally and physically, deprived by the loss of her

baby of everything that could give hope. Then, as she lay alone on the bed in her squalid little room, she had a kind of vision:

> Then my pain began to disappear. My body was free, as if I suddenly became divided into two. One part floated and the other remained in bed. "Finally," I murmured and felt a smile on my lips. I felt so light, as I had never felt before, and saw Him there, there on the ceiling. There was a luminous cross in a shade of green, with a little flame in the center. It seemed as though it were incorporating me into it. I didn't feel my painful body any more. . . . This was what I had been waiting for all my life. My happiness had no bounds, it is impossible to explain the degree of joy I reached. It lasted several minutes.

Then a neighbor called to her that her father had come to see her. All the joy vanished, though he embraced her and clearly was anxious about her. But his presence reasserted all the old "not O.K." feelings which he had pressed into her very soul from babyhood. She struggled, protesting at his scorn for the tiny room, which was her only personal territory. But the Parent was too strong, she gave in, as women in Mexico are trained to do. And her experience of freedom (from the squalor and the pain, and from the shameful body itself) faded, for she had no way to understand it, no way to act on it. The experience took a form that had no verbal content, unlike that of the three "converts" described earlier, whose minds naturally allowed them to some extent to verbalize the meaning of what happened, even at the time, though the experience transcended words. Because Consuelo's religious experience could not draw on any intellectual content with which to clothe itself, it was purely symbolic. The luminous, flame-centered cross recalls the mandala, one of the great cosmic symbols of wholeness and maturity, but it is also linked to the colorful, highly emotional, religious culture of Mexico, which has little to do with Christianity, and in Consuelo's mind consisted of a mixture of folk-magic, a vague but painful desire for transcendent experience or supernatural comfort, and morbid fantasies connected with death and sex. Whether the "Him" that Consuelo saw was actually an image of Christ, or whether she identified him with the luminous cross, it is hard to tell. Either way she had seen and felt the divine presence. She had had, in fact, a familiar kind of mystical experience, the "out-of-the-body" experience, and it was somehow focused on the mandala, the sign of wholeness. But the mystical teachers teach their pupils to use such an experience, to study it, and go on to the stage of spiritual growth proper to it. Poor Consuelo had no teacher, only her father to drag her back to where she began, more hopelessly "not O.K." than ever. And as far as one can tell, the experience left no trace, except as a wistful, painful nostalgia for the unattainable. As a little girl, she had gone to catechism classes, full of joy and hope. Then the catechist left the district, and there was no one to turn to. Later, she vaguely wanted to be a nun, sensing that this might be the gesture which would permit her to break free. But a friend told her (rightly or wrongly) she would need a dowry, and there was no chance of that. At least as far as the book goes, Consuelo is left without hope. Cheated and exploited by men she thought would help her out of her rut, she drifted into semi-prostitution—neurotic, desperate, without self-respect. That was what her Parent script had laid down for her, from the time she could walk, and the illumination that might have freed her had no effect, for she had no language with which to explain it.

Language is what the Parent gives, and language can decide the outcome. Another language may be substituted for the Parent one, if the converting "agent" has a clear and powerful language ready at hand. In the case of Elizabeth Fry, the Quaker speech literally gave her a new language, which did not obliterate the other—there was no need for that—but which gave her a new dimension of thought in which to live and understand her new self. The "thee's" of the Quakers, the special words—"concern," "to have a meeting"—the titles of Brother and Sister, were very powerful in detaching her from whatever in her old life she felt to be incompatible with her vocation. "It makes me think before I speak, and avoid the spirit of gaiety and flirting." But apart from the use of special words and phrases, specifically non-Parent ones, to mark and symbolize the new life, language is the broader sense of a whole way of thinking and feeling, and therefore of acting. As we have seen, the Parent language is vital, and ideally a large part of it should be incorporated into the new life, without any danger of backsliding—provided the awakened Adult is in charge of the process of change. When the Parent language is largely or wholly unsuitable for "conversion," a new one must be found, equally coherent, which the Adult can use to interpret and decide. The liberated Child cannot do this. The Child is at least partly preverbal, and what verbalization there is is poetic—that is, it expresses and celebrates feeling and spiritual desire. It cannot interpret or draw conclusions or decide on action. That was why Consuelo had no way to "use" her experience, which in itself was as valid as any of those recorded by great saints and mystics.

When a strong, new language is available, it can completely take the place of the Parent language, but it sometimes happens that the influence that brought about the liberation of the Child is itself a Child-contaminated one. That is, the Adult side of the new life—the sect or the person who converts—is not fully rational, but is using Adult thought processes under the command not of the Parent, but of the Child, and this can have very odd results. The Jesus People and similar groups that have converted so many youngsters in the United States use a language that is strongly biblical and definitely anti-intellectual.

The Adult is only allowed to "speak" in biblical words and
concepts, and every aspect of life is controlled by these
terms. In a way, the Bible becomes what might be called a
"Foster Parent." But the experience of liberation is in
many cases just as real and true, and the adolescents (often
drug addicts or completely disoriented people) are truly
converted. Here is a description of one such convert and of
an ocean baptism:

> He sat on the edge of the stage, barefoot, jeans and
> mod shirt, long hair. His face looked heavenward, and
> tears rolled off his cheeks. He laughed, he cried. He
> was crammed with emotion he couldn't explain or
> control. It whirlwinded him, erupted from him. The
> girl beside him understood. Her arm lightly over his
> shoulders, she comforted him. "I'm so happy for you,"
> she said. "I've been praying for you for two months."
> He turned to her, overwhelmed, awed, blitzed by in-
> tense feelings and joy. He shook his head. Laughing,
> the words tumbled out: "It's so wild . . . so wild . . .
> praise the Lord!"
>
> . . . . They're washed clean, these kids. Clean and
> pure. Jesus has washed away their sins. And they
> glow, faces alight in the joy and rapture of the moment
> they've wonderfully embraced. Dripping wet, clothes
> clinging to their bodies, salt water beading on their
> flushed faces, they emerge to be swallowed up
> again—by the loving arms of their friends.

The language is emotive, perhaps too much so, yet the
truth of the experience is attested to by many others, and it
is worth recording that a reporter and photographer who
were sent by a national magazine to do a feature story on
the Jesus People ended up by being converted themselves.

Often the families of such converts are like the one in

the first chapter, afraid to make decisions or exercise discipline, relying on a "what will the neighbors say" or "you'll break your mother's heart" type of moral blackmail. The previous escape into drugs, or sex, was not a liberation of the anxious and bewildered "not O.K." Child, but a frantic search for the "stroking" (comfort and reassurance) which the real parents did not give. The "conversion" occurs when the intense conviction of some "militant" manages to get through to the Child with a voice more powerful than his own fears. The Parent voices are, in any case, weak and ineffective in such people. But in some groups the Adult scarcely comes on the scene at all. A sort of Collective Child takes over, using the Bible as Foster Parent, as I suggested. Since, on the whole, the Bible is full of sensible and hopeful and "saving" doctrine, this can be a good thing, but it is extremely risky, all the same. The typical "fundamentalist" tendency to take texts of the Bible with absolute literalness can produce cruel and even lethal results. In the thirteenth century, the Cathari took the command "he that loses his life for my sake shall find it" to the point of committing suicide by starvation. Nowadays, the literal acceptance of a (badly translated Greek) New Testament sentence as an order to "hate your father and mother" can lead to brutal rejection of family ties, with more than a touch of unconscious revenge. (It is typical of the Child that it takes statements literally and out of context.)

There are degrees, of course. Many of these sects do, in practice, have leaders with a good functioning Adult that can interpret biblical concepts in a human and truthful way, so that in many cases such conversions do a lot of good, and lead to proper spiritual development. But it all depends on the interpretation of the almighty Foster Parent, and a danger does exist, as we shall see, especially in the case of "fake" conversions.

Where the Foster Parent is not the Bible but an influence of itself evil and corrupting, the disastrous results of such "conversions" are limitless. To the demoralized German nation, Hitler offered a "saving doctrine" so powerful in its appeal to anxious, insecure, and humiliated people that it completely "knocked out" the Parent, at least for the time being. In its place there came the Child, liberated, certainly—but liberated for evil. For part of the Child is what Eric Berne calls the "little Fascist" in each one of us, the vestigial destroyer and torturer-for-fun, who is normally kept under control, but waits for an opportunity to get to work. The language that defined and guided that conversion was the crazy language of the Adult entirely "contaminated" and used by the Fascist Child, so that the Child had gone berserk. (I suspect that the original "berserker" warriors may have been specially and virtually licensed Fascist-Child-people, but they were under the control of a strong Communal Parent, who could recall them to order.) The horrors of the Nazi torture chambers and camps, the unspeakable "experiments" and the wholesale massacres, are, on a huge scale, exactly the reaction one expects from a frightened and brutalized small child suddenly given the chance of an outing for his "little Fascist." When such a "Child" is "let out" in grown-up life, released from control of the Parent ("To kill is wrong," "You mustn't be cruel") without any intervening Adult, the results are frightful. When that sequence of events happens in many hundreds of cases, and when many others belong to the group of "false conversions" I shall be studying below, or else are too frightened and bewildered to do anything but keep quiet, you get the hell of Hitler's Germany. Hitler made himself Foster Parent to a whole culture, but the voice of that Foster Parent was not an Adult one; it was the voice of a crazy Child.

All these kinds of "conversion," even the evil ones, are "genuine." That is, the "not O.K." Child is assured of salvation. God (or something that did duty for God) said "You're O.K." The Child was liberated from the control of the Parent. What followed depended to a great extent, as we saw, on the type of "language" available—pure Parent, or Adult, or Child-contaminated Adult, or Adult-controlled Parent, or a mixture. But there is "false" conversion, too. It must be clear that by "false" I do not mean "bad in its effects." It can be good, just as a "genuine" conversion can be bad in its effects. The "falseness" of a "false" conversion consists in the fact that the Child is not really liberated, but rather, having struggled, it surrenders to the Parent, who then comforts and "strokes" it, producing feelings of great peace and "goodness." This is why it is sometimes hard to tell genuine from false. In the case of Nazi Germany, it seems likely that many of those who wept and screamed and fainted at the Führer's great speeches were, like the children of the Evangelical revival, discovering the bliss and peace of the Parent's full approval.

It is difficult, in practice, to define the noticeable differences between "true" and "false" conversion, since the "language" of both may be the same. If, for instance, the young evangelists of the Jesus movement are expecting a real "change" in their hearers, both types of converts will learn to express what has happened to them in the same terms, claiming Jesus as savior and life. But in some cases Jesus is the voice of the Parent, forgiving transgressions against the Parental code and welcoming back the errant Child to a life of sweet obedience with plenty of emotional rewards. The Adult is severely excluded from this transaction, which takes the form of the Child saying "I'm not O.K., forgive me," and the Parent saying "You can be O.K. if you're sorry." The Adult would upset this game. This accounts for the anti-intellectual nature of much fundamentalist religion, and of some types of piety encouraged among laypeople and nuns in Catholic and Episcopalian churches in the last century.

A contemporary example of this kind of thing refers to the very Parent-dominated fundamentalist group called Children of God that worked mainly in Texas until recently. They emphasize "100 per cent commitment," complete withdrawal from contact with the outside world, which is "idolatrous." Rules are strict and rigidly enforced. This group was called in to advise another "Jesus" group, which appears to have been genuinely searching for the freedom of Christ and a gospel-oriented life. This latter group was tackling difficulties of relationships, money, and organization, as any group must do which is both new and flexible and genuinely trying to discover the truth with its Adult. The Adult knows it does not know all the answers but, to the very young, this is disturbing. They feel a nostalgia for the Parent, who *knows,* and who can "stroke." These young people longed for strong, firm guidance. They did not have enough confidence in their Adult guidance of the Child's desires and dreams. So they called in (naturally enough) another group that seemed to have found answers and used the Gospel language with certainty and success. David, their leader, asked the Children of God to come and tell them all about it. This is how Walker Knight (in *Jesus People Come Alive*) described what happened next:

> They moved in with the hard sell, using video-tape replays of their national ministries, an uncompromising call to total commitment, and near-brainwashing techniques (one girl said she lost track of the days) with chants, yells, study and prayer that often had the kids near exhaustion with emotion and weariness. Eventually David and about eighty young people transferred to the new organization. . . . Visitors now find a changed atmosphere; they are stopped at the living room, and all visits with personnel are chaperoned.

The technique is familiar—the Adult is undermined by fatigue and inchoate sensations, then the "not O.K." Child is offered refuge and peace through surrender. But the aftereffects are far from the soaring, open-hearted freedom of true conversion. This type of "convert" will be very much wrapped up in the experience; nothing else will seem important. Such people are the reason for the frequent objections to "charismatic" or "revivalist" religion—namely, that it makes them oblivious to social injustice, careless of the larger demands of the Gospel while cherishing their own "experience." It is one big reason for the rejection of religion by social reformers and revolutionaries.

Where a real liberation takes place, however, the Child is set free, and becomes more active and outgoing in service to others, or sometimes, for those with a mystical type of personality, in prayer. The Gospel command to "leave all and follow me," to "go and teach all nations" is addressed to such people, because the energy and enthusiasm of the liberated Child are available under the command of the strong, observant Adult. This change may use the same type of "language," but in some cases, when conversion takes place in a context where the "new life" has insufficient scope, the results of conversion will lead the person outside the group in which it takes place. The Adult senses that the available "language" does not fully express what the liberated Child is wanting and needing. This is the impulse that produces movements of religious reform or revolt, led by a truly converted person for whom the existing Church setup is too narrowly Parent-ruled.

If the language of conversion is often adaptable to a false conversion, there are other signs that make the difference much clearer. The impulse to *do* something about the new life is one, but this again springs from a difference at the heart of the experience, and it has to do with repentance.

"Repent, and be baptized!" cried John the Forerunner, and Jesus sent out his own disciples to bid men repent, for the Kingdom of Heaven was at hand. "Repent and confess your sins" was the formula, and that really meant the same as "Be converted and publicly discard your sins," which is what happened. The early days of the church were marked

by that kind of "repentance," which meant a joyful acceptance of the salvation offered by Jesus. This involved a
public act of repudiation of the past, with its "bondage to
sin," and these conversions were sometimes accompanied
by tears. But the tears were the tears that people weep who
are released from fear and tension. They were not tears of
guilt. Peter wept tears of guilt after he had disowned his
master. He was appalled to find that his real love, his own
earlier conversion, still left him capable of Parent-impressed
fear of authority to the extent of denying the meaning of that
conversion. That was repentance in the modern sense,
which means sorrow for sin, real or imaginary. In practice,
there is no sharp dividing line. The convert may weep for
sheer joy of liberation, but may, at the same time, feel acutely
the memory of behavior that now, in the light of the new
experience, seems quite monstrous. But although this is
painful it is not a burden—on the contrary, it is a healthy pain
like the ache of muscles newly exercised after long illness. It
is recovery that makes their feeble condition apparent.

The weeping and anguish of the revivalist convert, however, like that of the children in the last chapter, is often
that of guilt only. The conviction of personal sinfulness
and its likely results (whether in terms of hell or simply of
personal degradation) is too much for the "not O.K." Child
to bear, and when the Parent offers release from this—on
conditions—the offer is accepted with a sense of enormous
relief. This relief is not the "freedom of the sons of God"
but is a handing-over of responsibility, a surrender to one
greater who will thereafter feed and console, always provided one conforms. And one of the conditions may be the
production of suitable signs of "conversion," as we have
seen. The confusion between "genuine" and "false" conversion is all the greater because the preacher of repentance may intend genuinely to bring people to the freedom of Christ, and the emphasis on sin and hell is
intended to show what a real liberation is being offered.
More confusing still, the agony of repentance may be what

is needed to shake the confidence of a person who has been for years comfortably embedded in the Parent "script," doing "the right thing." The preaching of sin, etc., may well be a prelude to genuine conversion when the newly insecure Child, missing the Parent but rejecting it, can "hear" the good news of real freedom. Before that, it might have fallen on deaf ears. And even when there is no violent upheaval, it is necessary that in some way the Parent should be "dethroned," and the "script" at least regarded with suspicion, before conversion can take place.

A book that has attained immense popularity in the last few years is the fictionalized biography of a young school-teacher in the early years of this century. (Written by the subject's daughter, though in the first person, *Christy*, by Catherine Marshall, has been published in the United States and in Europe, and has gone into several paperback printings.) The style and approach sometimes verge on the sentimental, which is a pity, because at the level of obser-vation and re-creation of experience it is extremely (even harshly) true to life. And because the life evoked is the crude, cruel, squalid, yet strong and beautiful life of the mountain people, the spiritual crises that arise are ines-capable, uncushioned by the pieties and evasions that might work in more urbane settings, and the various kinds of spiritual encounter are more easily recognizable.

The story of one year in the life of Christy Huddleston, a feminine, idealistic, and well-brought-up girl from a loving home, shows very clearly the various types of "repen-tance" and conversion. The first one happens when Christy, brought up by her parents to respect "charity" and admire courage and dedication, hears an appeal by a missionary for someone to teach the children in a remote mountain community. Christy's response to this call is ro-mantic and starry-eyed, and has full Parent approval (which is what she wants) even though the real parents are worried and doubtful about the decision. But their wor-ries, of course, are satisfying to the slightly rebellious

Child, who is saying (behind her hand) "This is what you said you wanted, *now* see how you like it!" The Child is wanting room, in fact, and the Adult feels the need for autonomy. None of this is conversion, but it is an important preliminary. The impulse is a good one, providing proper opportunities for growth of the Adult and exercise of the Child, even though it is still firmly under Parent control.

The conditions of life at Cutter Gap, however, are not the kind that sustain romantic impulse at that level. Christy comes up against dirt, mental illness, crude cruelty, and lethal superstitions. In the face of it, she nearly gives up and goes home. She goes to see Miss Alice, a Quaker woman who has worked in the area for years, and tells her she cannot stand it any more. Miss Alice forces her to look at her own motives and recognize that against real evil, second-hand conviction (i.e., the need for the approval of the Parent) is not enough.

> You see, Christy, evil is real—and powerful. It has to be fought, not explained away, not fled. And God is against evil all the way. So each of us has to decide where *we* stand, how we're going to live *our* lives. . . . It's late and you're tired. But here's the question for you to sleep on: were you supposed to come here, Christy? Or were you just running away from home?

In other words: Did your Adult make the decision to come here, because this work would provide scope for your "O.K." Child to work, too? Or was it just the "not O.K." Child running away from the hurt of unfulfilled Parent expectations? Next day, Christy feels better, because, first, Miss Alice's kindness and warmth had reassured the "not O.K." Child, and second, the Adult is always more in control after a good night's rest, especially if the Child is pleased and comforted by the sunshine of a bright spring morning. Such exterior things can make an important difference, as everyone can verify.

So she stays and works hard, but meets her next testing when she has, all on her own, made an expedition to town and persuaded some wealthy businessmen to give books and equipment to the impoverished mission. The day after the lovely new books have been displayed in the school-room, she comes in to find them all trampled, torn, and slashed. She questions the children, but cannot find the culprit, and when an older, very stupid and "mean" boy defies her, she loses her temper and screams at him. She is rescued from his violent reaction by David, the young minister at the mission. Next day they talk to Miss Alice, who fills the role of therapist in the story, as people like her so often do. She makes Christy realize *why* she was so angry:

> I believe it was because the new books were a prod-
> uct of your latest brain-child, thoughtfully conceived,
> brought to birth with flair and success. . . . True, you
> undertook the trip to Knoxville to help other people,
> but self went, self wore a ravishing hat, self sold her
> cause to an interesting wealthy man. . . ."

The use of the metaphor of childbirth is revealing. The "self" that went to Knoxville was "Daddy's darling," the appealing "little girl" whom her father adored and in-dulged and who responded with all the tricks of feminine charm. No wonder the destruction of the books won by that "sweet little girl" made the Child take over in rage and chagrin, reacting just as the three-year-old Christy might have reacted to a little boy who cut off the hair of the doll her father had given her. But the real point of Christy's experience, as Miss Alice points out, is that it contains a valuable lesson for her Adult. And to explain this she uses the image of a baby learning to walk, who falls, and if nobody is watching, gets up without fuss and goes on again. The Adult is awakening even in the one-year-old, and he tries, and goes on trying, to conquer obstacles and cope with himself—unless there is someone there to encourage the Child to produce a "poor little me" reaction, appealing for comfort and cuddles, or else a rage at the "naughty floor." (Some parents actually foster this by smacking the "naughty floor" or table, or by consoling and petting a baby in no need of consolation.) But all babies fall, and so does the Child in the grown-up person. The Adult knows this and gets up and goes on, but it is much easier to take refuge in the Child, blaming others and using failure as an excuse for not trying again. Worse still, however, is the conviction fostered by the Parent that one *cannot* fail without losing "self-respect" (i.e., Parent approval), and so some way must be found for seeing it *not* as failure, but a triumph of "sensitivity" or "integrity" or "common sense." Against both of these, Miss Alice guards Christy.

> "Well, the baby can teach us. What you've undertaken . . . isn't a state of perfection to be arrived at all of a sudden. It's a *walk*, and a walk isn't static but ever-changing. . . . Wallowing in self-condemnation or feeling sorry for yourself is worse than falling on your face in the first place. So—thee fell into a temper! So thee is human. Thank God for thy humanness."

All this shakes up confidence in the Parent script and encourages the Adult to control the Child reactions to Parent chagrin when something goes wrong. Other things shake the Parent, too, as when the atheist doctor in the Cove challenges Christy to say what *she* believes, and all she can do is quote Miss Alice, because she cannot rake up any real Adult-discovered and -expressed conviction of her own. This experience still further loosens the hold of her

"script" and produces real "repentance," that is, an awareness of the uselessness of the Parent script for real, personal decision, to meet the kind of circumstances the
script did not cover. The usual way to deal with this is to
"duck"—to avoid such circumstances as "not for me." But
Christy (among—happily—many others) is rescued from
that by the "therapist," in this case Miss Alice. So she has
to face her own inadequacy, and it is fully revealed when
her best friend in the Cove dies. This is the beautiful,
uneducated but sensitive and deeply poetic Fairlight
Spencer, "a princess in homespun" as Christy calls her,
whose delight in life and in all beauty inspires Christy,
and who is in turn inspired to reach out for more knowledge, through Christy. Fairlight dies during a typhoid epi-
demic, leaving a family of small children, and Christy's
script-inspired confidence and Parent-type religion is finally shattered. It is all so pointless! Those children need
their mother, her husband needs her, and her lovely spirit
was just beginning to blossom in new ways. What a futile
waste! She rages at God, who has turned out not to be the
indulgent, supportive, understanding Father-Parent that
she had counted on. David, the young minister, evades her
questions about "afterlife" with neat "liberal-Christian"
formulas about the rhythm of nature and death being "a
very great mystery." And he tries to distract her with lovemaking, appealing to her Child. This might have worked
earlier, but the process of repentance had gone too far for
that. In her desperation she seeks solitude, and is at least
able to reproach God, consciously and without pretense,
no longer tied by a Parent-type religion that depends on
pretending that one approves of God's curious behavior,
one which in anyone else would be thought abominable.
This agony of separation from the supporting-Parent is the
real repentance. The honesty of the writers of the Psalms
shows this change from Parent religion to true repentance
and the painful conflict it entails:

Yet thou hast cast us off and abased us,
    And hast not gone out with our armies . . .
Thou hast made us the taunt of our neighbours,
    the derision and scorn of those about us . . .
All day long my disgrace is before me,
    and shame has covered my face . . . .
All this has come upon us, though we have not forgotten
    thee,
    or been false to thy covenant.
Our heart has not turned back, nor have our steps
    departed from thy way,
that thou shouldst have broken us in the place
    of jackals, and covered us in deep darkness. . . .
Rouse thyself! Why sleepest thou, O Lord?
    Awake! Do not cast us off forever!
Why dost thou hide thy face?
    Why dost thou forget our affliction and oppression?
For our soul is bowed down to the dust;
    our body cleaves to the ground.
Rise up! Come to our help! [Psalm 44 RSV]

It seems so unjust that the Parent-God who has been so
faithfully obeyed should let us down! If we had been
naughty, that at least would seem reasonable to the Child,
but we've been so good! Yet this "being good," this effort
to "keep the law" of the Parent-God really is the necessary
preliminary, provided that what is "Parent-God" of one
generation has at some time been the God who liberates
the Child and enables the Adult. This idea needs to be
pursued further in the next chapter; it is enough at the
moment to determine that it is so. The Parent-God's commands, properly followed by the Adult, prepare the
ground for the full freedom. And the obedient servant of
the Parent-God can, with right on his side, complain to his
God and demand his help in his trouble. Fair enough,
since it is His fault! This outraged yet confident cry for
help, which is more like a command, is a sort of permis-

sion to the Child to respond to the Liberator-God. This is what happens in Christy's case, after days and days of desolate, angry questioning and demand. As Miss Alice tells her:

". . . those who've never rebelled against God or at some point in their lives shaken their fists in the face of heaven, have never encountered God at all."
  "You mean it's good to rebel?"
  ". . . I mean that rebellion against our human lot and admitting we don't understand are clear steps on the way to facing reality."

The reality is God, but a very different God from the indulgent, respectable, comprehensible Daddy of her upbringing and her conventional religious concepts:

Morning after morning I returned to my hillside . . . to . . . a silence so complete it seemed palpable, sensate, an entity in itself. Yet the quietness was no sterile emptiness. Those who craved oblivion could not have tolerated this. Or those who wanted to escape from themselves would flee this. . . . For now I knew that at the heart of the stillness there was food to feed upon, wisdom to accept humbly. . . .
  And slowly, almost imperceptibly, out of the stillness during that second week my answer started coming—only not in any way I expected. No effort was made to answer my "why?" Instead, I began to know, incredibly, unmistakably, beyond reason and doubting that I, Christy Huddleston, was loved— tenderly, totally. Love filled me, washed over me, flowed around me. I did not know what to do with love as strong as this. Back off from its intensity? Embrace it?
  My tears flowed. I could not stop them.
  . . . . The world around me was still full of riddles

for which my little mind had not been given answers. . . . Nor could I know what the future held.
But the fundamental doubt was for me silenced. I
knew now, God *is*. I had found my center, my point of
reference. Everything else I needed to know would
follow.

That morning the sun came up in a blaze of glory.

If the language seems like "novelist's language" we
have only to remember the descriptions of converted teen-
agers, their faces wet with tears of happiness and glowing
new awareness. But this semifictional conversion is not a
"lightning" one, but a gradual unfolding to completeness,
like that of Elizabeth Gurney. Elizabeth also found that
"everything else" she needed to know would follow, because the Adult now has its "point of reference" and can
deal with real situations in accordance with real standards
that give scope for the development of the whole person.
The future development is implicit in the moment of revelation—provided the right kind of language is available

We can see this working even when the language is only
half-understood, and gropingly, laboriously interpreted by
the Adult. In Graham Greene's *End of the Affair,* Sarah is
married to a kind, boring, impotent civil-servant whom she
does not love. She has the "Affair" of the title with
Maurice, a selfish, possessive young writer, who both
wants her and cannot help trying to hurt her all the time.
His jealousy cannot bring itself to believe in her truth-
fulness and honesty. For Sarah, completely realistic about
herself, knows herself for "a bitch and a fake." She never
tries to pretend that her love affair is a triumph for freedom or a "realistic" way of handling her sex life. She simply loves Maurice, is hurt by him, and hates herself. Her
mother is a self-deceiving, self-righteous woman who is
always being "let down" or "misunderstood" by men, who
are all "mean." She wanted revenge on them, especially
her first husband, and used the baby Sarah for this pur-

pose, having the child secretly baptized against her husband's wishes—though she herself "didn't *believe* much." So Sarah's Mother-Parent impressions add up to a "script" ordering a career of deception, not-being-loved, secretiveness, and being optimistic but inefficient in personal relationships. But the Child-dominated mother evidently stimulated in Sarah as well as all this a wistful, hopeful, truly loving "natural" Child, responding to the one that was present (though distorted by "not O.K." rationalizations) in the mother, too. And it is this hopeful and enthusiastic Child in Sarah who longs for "something"—*love*, beauty, a future—in what is in most respects a reasonably sordid and self-centered "love" affair. Perhaps her *awareness* of her pretenses and disloyalty, something her mother would never have managed, is made possible by a strong Adult, activated by the practical need to cope with the vagaries of the Child in her mother. So Sarah's repentance is real and runs side by side with what her Parent would regard as her "sin," because real repentance—the kind that leads to genuine conversion—is awareness of helplessness and failure, not mere self-disgust (Parent-inspired) at particular kinds of behavior. Self-disgust, as we saw, can easily lead to self-pity and a retreat to the Parent, who scolds but protects. Christy almost did this, but was shown the way ahead by the "therapist" who intervened. The "therapist" in Sarah's case is not a person but a complex of converging circumstances—vaguely "religious" feelings and reactions, mainly superstitions implanted by her mother, and the falling of a bomb. Maurice and Sarah have been making love in his flat during an air raid; they decide to go down to the basement for safety, but not if anyone else is there, so Maurice goes down first to see. While he is in the hall a bomb falls nearby. He is knocked over by the blast, pinned down by the front door. It is never clear in the book whether he actually dies or whether Sarah—touching his hand protruding from under the debris—merely thinks he does. But she, at least, is convinced of his death. She goes back to the bedroom and, kneeling naked on the floor, vows that if God will restore him to life she will leave him. It is a genuine, agonized reaching-out to the living God, expressed in terms of childish religious ideas learned from a mother who did not even believe. In the diary she writes later she recalls what she felt, telling herself, as she writes, that "I mustn't break down because I must protect Henry" (as, earlier, she had protected her mother) and protesting,

> I want somebody who'll accept the truth about me and doesn't need protection. . . . I knelt down on the floor: I was mad to do such a thing: I never even had to do it as a child—my parents never believed in prayer, any more than I do. I hadn't any idea what to say. Maurice was dead. Extinct. There wasn't such a thing as a soul. . . . He would never have the chance to be happy again.

Sarah's father was an unbeliever—a condition of her conversion is her rejection of his commands, by kneeling down to pray, and her Father-Parent fights back in the language of rationalism. But the astute Child is skilled in the technique of the "anti-script" and uses this very prohibition to get free. The tense struggle of the natural Child for freedom, arguing with the Parent, and appealing to that vague omnipotent Therapist she doesn't believe in, works through to freedom and peace, but at enormous cost, because the superstitious religious Parent-language demands "payment" for liberation. The sacrifice can be, and is, liberating, but the confused religious language makes it seem arbitrary, ridiculous, the demand of a false "Parent-God" who takes bribes. This misery and confusion destroys the joy that should accompany conversion; Sarah does not know "everything else I needed to know," but has therefore to discover it, bit by bit, with her Adult. All the same, there is real repentance.

I knelt and put my head on the bed and wished I could believe. Dear God, I said—why dear, why dear?—make me believe. I can't believe. Make me. I said, I'm a bitch and a fake and I hate myself. I can't do anything of myself. . . . *Make* me believe. I shut my eyes tight, and I pressed my nails into the palms of my hands until I could feel nothing but the pain, and I said, I will believe. Let him be alive, and I *will* believe. Give him a chance. . . . But that wasn't enough. It doesn't hurt to believe. So I said, I love him and I'll do anything if you'll make him alive. I said very slowly, I'll give him up for ever, only let him be alive with a chance. . . . People can love without seeing each other, can't they, they love You all their lives without seeing You, and then he came in at the door, and he was alive, and I thought now the agony of being without him starts. . . .

Here, the link between repentance and sacrifice is apparent. Is it just an Old Testament idea, the need to placate a jealous God with presents? Is the idea of painful sacrifice merely a morbid perversion of religion, the Parent punishing the rebellious Child, and afterwards taking him back "forgiven"? It is easy to overlook the sacrifice element in a conversion whose main characteristic is joy, yet in the story of Christy, conversion could only take place when the approval of the Parent had been—very painfully—sacrificed. Pascal had to abandon his reliable, mathematical Parent, and fought hard not to. Betsy Gurney had much to give up which was obviously good and beautiful before her natural Child could be free and joyful. Sarah's sacrifice of physical lovemaking and the presence of her lover is, for her, the necessary prelude to genuine conversion, because her love affair represented a bondage to her script, which laid down that she was to love "mean" men and be misunderstood. The sacrifice is the "death" of her script-life, and is therefore a saving sacrifice. But, for

her, the element of joy is scarcely noticeable, being so
overlaid with confusion of mind and the pain of the "not
O.K." Child's continuing desire for comfort. The liberation
is real, but not complete. For a long time, Sarah still struggles to persuade herself that the experience, and therefore
the commitment, are not real. She tries to get involved
with other men, she talks to an atheist, hoping to be convinced. She *is* convinced—that there is God. So she goes
to a priest, to see if she can find a "religious" way out of
her commitment, but that does not work. In the end she
gives in, her Parent is defeated, but although she finds
peace she cannot find happiness, and death comes to complete the work she could not achieve otherwise. Her last
letter to her lover is delayed in the post and arrives after
her death:

> . . . I believe there's a God—I believe the whole bag
> of tricks, there's nothing I don't believe, they could
> subdivide the Trinity into a dozen parts and I'd be-
> lieve. They could dig up records that proved Christ
> had been invented by Pilate to get himself promoted
> and I'd believe just the same. I've caught belief like a
> disease. I've fallen into belief like I fell in love. I've
> never loved before as I loved you, and I've never be-
> lieved in anything before as I believe now. I'm sure.
> I've never been sure before about anything. When you
> came in at the door with the blood on your face, I
> became sure. Once and for all. Even though I didn't
> know it at the time. I fought belief for longer than I
> fought love, but I haven't any fight left. Maurice. . . .
> I used to think I was sure about myself and what was
> right and wrong, and you taught me not to be sure.
> You took away all my lies and self-deceptions like
> they clear a road of rubble for somebody to come
> along it, somebody of importance . . . and now he's
> come. . . ."

Which, being interpreted, means that Maurice, who loved and hated, unleashed that repentance by the blows of his hatred which were accepted in love. Sexual love can do this. The closeness of a passionate relationship brings people up against the reality of themselves just as, for Christy, the vice and violence and squalor of mountain life left no room for pretenses. "Romantic" sex really means the sexual expression of the "natural" Child, seeking freedom with the strong help of another's love. The lover sends the Parent packing, while at the same time reassuring the "not O.K." Child that it is safe and cherished. But of course the majority of conversions that happen because of this kind of love do not use a "religious" language to describe what happens, they use a sexual one, a "falling-in-love" language, which may or may not include a "marriage" vocabulary. The conversion is just as real, the Child is released and finds joy, creativity, and hope, but what happens next depends on the kind of ideas the two people, and their "society," have about falling in love. So if their society says "love equals marriage," they marry. If their society (maybe among the medieval "Romance" groups, or a group that is "anti-establishment") says "Marriage is an empty legal formality that oppresses women," then they may just live together. At another time when frustrated love was the great emotional experience, they may sometimes have preferred to be separated by parents, class, illness, etc., and suffer pangs of unappeased passion. In any case, the falling-in-love experience is regarded as crucial in their lives, and it really is a proper "conversion."

We can see it happening very clearly in one of the most famous of love stories, Jane Austen's *Pride and Prejudice*, a good example because it is so well known, and also because the "P.A.C." setup is so easily recognizable. Elizabeth Bennet has her father's witty and cynical style; she dislikes people easily and is very critical. "Prejudice" is the Parent quality par excellence. But she has her mother's

happy disposition, which comes through in her in a pleasant way, because her mother was probably at her best as a
younger mother, being Child with her own small children.
At other times Mrs. Bennet's unvarying Child is unbeara-
bly silly. (She must have been the kind of sweet little girl
whose father constantly told her "Don't bother your pretty
little head with serious things! Just enjoy yourself and
Papa will take care of you!") But Elizabeth and her elder
sister Jane possess plenty of Adult, possibly because of
having had to cope with a remarkably silly mother from an
early age and to protect themselves and the rest of the family from the ravages of her ups and downs and indiscre-
tions.

Darcy, on the other hand, says of himself, "As a child, I
was taught what was *right;* but not taught to correct my
temper. . . . Unfortunately, an only son . . . I was spoiled
by my parents, who, though good themselves . . . allowed, encouraged, almost taught me to be selfish and
overbearing—to care for none beyond my own family circle, to think meanly of all the rest of the world. . . ."

Naturally, when they meet he is appalled at her mother's
vulgarity, and the fine reproduction of it in the two youngest
girls. (They have never had to cope with their mother, their
elders did that, and their father's message to them is "You are
like your mother!"). He treats Elizabeth with disdain and
—far worse—proceeds to remove his friend Bingley from his
growing relationship with Elizabeth's lovely elder sister,
Jane. Elizabeth, already angry at his reputation and manners, really hates him after this, and cannot say or hear too
much ill of him. So she easily falls for the charm of the
rascally Wickham, who tells lies about Darcy in order to
show himself in a pathetic light.

Darcy's conversion proceeds faster than Elizabeth's.
First attracted because she does not toady to him, he
learns to admire her wit, then her love and concern for her
sister when she is ill. Finally, when she is staying near the
mansion of his colossally arrogant and vulgar aunt (she is a

caricature of Darcy's worst faults), he proposes to her, never doubting for a moment that she will be over-whelmed with gratitude and pleasure at such an offer from such a man—especially when he tells her how hard he found it to overcome his repugnance to her family! But Elizabeth refuses him with fury. She tells him, at the end of a stormy interview during which she accuses him of ruining Wickham's prospects and her own sister's happi-ness, that "You are mistaken, Mr. Darcy, if you suppose that the mode of your declaration affected me in any other way, than as it spared me the concern which I might have felt in refusing you, had you behaved in a more gentle-manlike manner."

This is a shattering blow to Darcy's powerful Parent, for it calls in question everything he has been taught to take for granted. He writes her a long letter, explaining how it was in fact Wickham's own lies and irresponsibility that spoiled his chances, and that he, Darcy, had genuinely believed he was acting for the best in regard to Jane and Bingley. He is not really repentant at the beginning of the letter—merely angry and anxious to justify himself. But the process of explanation brings a change, as he realizes how his behavior may look to others. As Darcy says later, "I am since convinced it was written in a dreadful bitter-ness of spirit," but Elizabeth replies, "The letter, perhaps, began in bitterness, but it did not end so. . . . " and Darcy adds that "my anger soon began to take a proper di-rection," that is, against himself. His conversion is progres-sing splendidly, he is truly repentant, but so far it is still partly the anger at unworthy behavior, not the realization of a new life.

Elizabeth's conversion is begun by reading the letter, which he hands to her next day. Being honest, she cannot refuse to listen to his arguments, however reluctantly at first. She soon realizes that his account of his relationship with Wickham bears the stamp of truth, and, on rereading the rest, begins to do him more justice. She sees that her prejudice (and her pleasure in flattery, which is her Mother-Parent egging on her Child) have led her both to like Wickham and dislike Darcy. "She grew absolutely ashamed of herself. Of neither Darcy nor Wickham could she think, without feeling that she had been blind, partial, prejudiced, absurd." Still, it is only self-blame, and even a little self-pity. The Parent is upset but not routed. Darcy, meanwhile, is well on the way to total conversion by facing up to himself. When the two meet accidentally in the grounds of his home ("open to visitors") he has reached the stage of wanting, with his Child, to show her he has changed, and a real, though not sudden, change takes place as he "acts" the change, for his internal image of Elizabeth as "therapist" is giving him permission to change and defy his Parent.

> My object *then* . . . was to show you, by every civility in my power, that I was not so mean as to resent the past; and I hoped to obtain your forgiveness [that is, to get assurance from her Adult that he was "O.K."] . . . by letting you see that your reproofs had been attended to. How soon any other wishes introduced themselves I can hardly tell, but I believe in about half an hour after I had seen you.

But so far the change is not complete. Darcy's Parent is still biding his time. After all, being "civil" is good Parent behavior; no radical sacrifice of pride has been made. Elizabeth, now, is further on than he. Humiliated, and accepting her own revealed foolishness and meanness, her Child is open to the newly displayed natural Child in Darcy. But the conversion is brought to a climax for both when news comes that Elizabeth's younger sister, Lydia, has eloped with Wickham and is living with him, unmarried, in London. This is Elizabeth's Parent's final defeat, for her father's cynical detachment and her mother's happy-go-lucky selfishness are both shown up for the disastrous influences they really are. Feeling that Darcy cannot possibly want to marry a member of a family thus disgraced, she now finally realizes how much she needs him to save her newly vulnerable but very loving Child and to support her Adult in managing her Parent.

Darcy, however, blames himself for the disaster, because he did not warn others of Wickham's character, being too proud to display his personal troubles. So he feels obliged to do what he can to help. He finds the couple, persuades (i.e., bribes) Wickham to marry Lydia, and attends her wedding. He does it secretly, not wishing to put the Bennets under an obligation to himself, but by involving himself deliberately in this sordid situation he is defying every Parental injunction. He dares to do this, because of his "therapist," Elizabeth, who is present "in his head" throughout, encouraging and reassuring. He still does not know whether she loves him, but his arrogant aunt settles that. Hearing rumors that Elizabeth is favored by Darcy, she calls on Elizabeth to tell her to leave her illustrious nephew alone. Elizabeth refuses to give any such assurance, and when Darcy hears this from his indignant aunt he posts off to confirm his hopes. All is explained, and happiness reigns. Poor Bingley is kindly allowed to love Jane again, for Darcy is to Bingley a Parent figure who can give such commands. But then Bingley is the kind of person who scarcely needs a "conversion." His script says "Be happy, please everybody, and always come out 'right.' " So everyone is happy, including Mrs. Bennet—presumably—since "the business of her life was to get her daughters married," probably on orders from her Father-Parent who must have been an insufferable, pompous autocrat, rather like Elizabeth's plain sister Mary, but (being male) able to be kind and condescending as well as priggish.

The temptation to pursue these avenues of analysis is almost irresistible, especially as they help to open up the subject, but this much analysis shows well enough how a sexual "conversion" can work. Many times, of course, there is no genuine conversion, but merely the surrender to the Parent in a new form, just as in some false religious conversion. Such is David Copperfield's marriage to the child-wife Dora, as like his child-mother as makes no difference.

Sometimes the conversion is genuine but takes place by disillusion, as in the case of Anne Frank. Her love for the boy shut up with her in their secret apartment where the two families hid from the Germans was at first a search for an alternative Parent to comfort her lonely Child. Her real parents were too anxious and afraid to help her. By realizing that he was fallible, weak, and needy himself, Anne came to self-understanding. Her Adult argued it out:

"A type like Peter finds it difficult to stand on his own feet, but it's even harder to stand on your own feet as a conscious, living being." (This is a very good description of the converted liberated self—autonomous, but still vulnerable). "Because if you do, then it's twice as difficult to steer a path through the sea of problems and still remain constant through it all. I'm just drifting around, have been searching for days, searching for a good argument against that terrible word 'easy.' . . ." Anne was unusually objective about herself, because her father had given her Adult permission to cope: "I understand more and more how true Daddy's words were when he said: 'All children must look after their own upbringing.' " But this attitude of his also left her unprotected, hence her sense of the "problems," and her felt need to be "constant." Her Parent was always telling her to find the "easy" way. But it was the fact that, at the crisis, her father "let her down" and could not understand or help that really opened her up and made her take over her own destiny. She rose out of the "sea of problems" and made her hard-won act of faith. She also expressed her kind of repentance, which meant rejecting the trend to acceptance and inertia in herself. It is so easy to justify such attitudes in a world of what she called "horrible truth." That way is not good, though it had always been her Parent's way:

> It's really a wonder that I haven't dropped all my ideals because they seem so absurd and impossible to carry out. Yet, I keep them, because in spite of everything I believe that people are really good at heart. I simply can't build my hopes on a foundation consisting of confusion, misery and death. I see the world gradually being turned into a wilderness, I hear the ever-approaching thunder, which will destroy us too, I can feel the sufferings of millions, and yet, if I look up into the heavens, I think that it will all come right, that this cruelty too will end, and that peace and tranquillity will return again.
>
> In the meantime, I must uphold my ideals, for perhaps the time will come when I shall be able to carry them out.

The time did come, only three weeks later, though not in the way she hoped. In the concentration camp to which she and her mother and sister were taken when the Nazis discovered their hiding place, Anne remained true to her conversion. Possibly it was only there that she fully realized it. A description of her by someone who was there refers to the shaven, emaciated teenager as "radiant." That is what conversion is about, for that first, untouched Child who comes into this world with "clouds of glory" can rediscover them as his natural element. Sometimes it happens in one great explosion of light and joy, leading to final freedom in martyrdom. More often it is a long, slow process, for the initial liberation is not total, there is much still to be done in sifting and discerning the Parent messages, in controlling and retraining the Adapted Child (the "not O.K." whiny, deceitful, or vicious one) and—most difficult—releasing and redirecting the impulses of the ancestral Child, which may be angelic or demonic according to the cultural setting in which one operates. All this has to be done by the Adult, powered by the liberated Child, and harking back to it. (We shall see how this harking back is done in the last chapter.)

So the question of the language the Adult uses, as we have seen, is crucial. For the completion of the process initiated by conversion is the part referred to by Elizabeth Fry as "knowing what to do." She herself had to wait a long time before the power of her conversion was allowed full scope in her work in Newgate, but when the time came she "knew what to do," and she knew what to do meanwhile, too. Paul realized that what he "had to do" was to go and preach to the Gentiles. Elizabeth Bennet (and others in that tradition) had instructions to get married and raise a family. They knew "what to do" with the liberated Child, so that the whole self could grow. Anne Frank "remained constant" to the end, believing "that people are really good at heart" in the one place and time of all history where it must have been hardest to believe anything of the sort. Sarah Miles vowed to live out her life without her love, for his sake. Pascal used his gifts to serve others and to fight ignorance and prejudice. Christy went out to carry on the same work, with a wholly new power and insight, and to recognize, also, the kind of man who could help her do it.

The "what to do" is not just a follow-up, it is an integral part of the whole development, but it cannot happen until there is a real "conversion" decision. After that, other decisions follow, always in relation to that. As Eric Berne puts it:

> There are hierarchies of decisions, and the highest level is the decision to follow or not to follow a script, and until that decision is made, all other decisions will not avail to change the individual's ultimate destiny. . . . Yet all levels contribute directly to the final

outcome, and are designed to bring it about more effectively, whether that is script-directed or autonomously chosen.

So when God, the great script-breaker, has set free the Child and made possible the new life of the autonomous self, there are still all the other decisions to be made, to make the Freedom "come true." The beginning is what Paul called a "babe in Christ"; he needs milk and support and lots of reassurance. Later, if all goes well, he will grow strong enough to stand alone, and also to help liberate others. But how it works, and how it grows, and if it grows depends on the language. The absence of any language at all can abort the experience completely, while an evil one can make its fruits monstrous. A limited "vocabulary" can restrict growth and virtually ensure that only certain aspects of life benefit from the conversion. This is true of many conversions that occur in a sexual language, whether this is a "free-love" language or a "marriage and domesticity" language. A language that emphasizes one aspect of the new life over all the others can distort the development, as is sometimes the case with Pentecostal sects, and even unbalanced emphasis on conversion itself can cause trouble. But a full, rich, subtle language can release the full power of the Spirit, and the result is the phenomenon we call sanctity.

> Unless you change and become like little children you will never enter the kingdom of heaven. [Mt. 18:3]
> Let the little children alone, and do not stop them coming to me; for it is to such as these that the kingdom of heaven belongs. [Mt. 19:14]

The words of Jesus are unequivocal, and we need only make them children with a capital 'C' to see the literal truth of this. What he wants is not the meek, obedient "adapted" Child, but the "natural" Child allied to the archetypal Child who was from the beginning:

Before the mountains were settled,
    before the hills, I came to birth;
before he made the earth, the countryside,
    or the first grains of the world's dust.
When he fixed the heaven firm, I was there. . .
    when he fixed fast the springs of the deep, . . .
I was by his side, a master craftsman,
    delighting him day after day,
    ever at play in his presence,
at play everywhere in his world,
    delighting to be with the sons of men. [Proverbs
      8:25–31]

The words are put into the mouth of the Wisdom of God, in the book of Proverbs, and they make clear the Child aspect of the Spirit, which is "at play" and "delighting" in God's new, wonderful world. This is the inheritance of Man, and of each human child. The curse that overshadows it and blots it out can be lifted, the script that enslaves can be broken. This is what the idea of "redemption" is about—the freeing of the enslaved by someone else. We have seen this happening in this chapter, and we have seen how important the "language" of the sequel must be. So it is not surprising that the Wisdom who plays in the new creation follows this up with an injunction to those "sons of men" to "listen to me, listen to instruction and learn to be wise." Wisdom, though in the Child, has to be learned, by "listening" to "instruction."

What kind of instruction, and how do we listen? That is the next question to be examined.

3

"On Earth as It Is in Heaven"

ONE of the biggest problems in understanding religious behavior (morality, ritual, and so on) is that the same kind of behavior can truly express a conversion, or be simply part of a Parent "script," hammered into the individual from an early age. So a person may, for instance, give hours every week to prison visiting, either out of genuine compassion and an outgoing love for other human beings who are suffering, or because the Parent (ministers, teachers, actual parents) said "You aren't a real Christian if you don't sacrifice yourself for others," or words to that effect.

It *is* possible to tell the difference, and "do-gooders" are easily distinguished from the ones who act out of love—that is, the "converted" ones, whose loving Child is free to "pour out my Spirit upon all flesh." A congregation in church will also contain, probably, only a small proportion of people for whom every word and gesture of the ritual is the expression of their own tremendous freedom and love. (This has little to do with their emotions, by the way—the

deeper it goes the less "surface disturbance" there will
be.) The rest will be the conscientious, obedient ones,
who are there because they have been told it is right.

Does that mean that no one should perform "acts of
charity" unless he truly "has charity"? Should we make
conversion a condition of church membership, as indeed
some sects to?

The answers are not so easy. After all, the man who
sends money to a charity in order to keep his Parent quiet
is benefiting just as many people as the one who does it
out of real love. (More, if he sends a bigger check.) At a
deeper level, the kind of behavior that belongs to a genuine religious tradition is actually good "education" for conversion, as well as an expression of it, when it has happened. Why? The reason is that the tradition (moral and
ritual) created by converted people is a "language" that
expresses what they "know" about life and love. This language is limited, externally, to what words and gestures
and judgments are available: they have to be words, actions, rules, that people can remember. They cannot,
therefore, fully express what the converted "know." So
there is room for misunderstanding, for "legalism" or just
plain hypocrisy to take the place of genuine experience.

Paul had a lot of trouble with people who thought obser-
vance was the important thing. They were always turning
up and trying to undo his work. Paul did not believe in
hiding his feelings, and he showed them clearly to his
misguided converts in Galatia:

Are you people in Galatia mad? Has someone put a
spell on you, in spite of the plain explanation you
have had of the crucifixion of Jesus Christ? Let me ask
you one question: Was it because you practiced the
Law that you received the Spirit, or because you believed what was preached to you? Are you foolish
enough to end in outward observances what you
began in the Spirit? . . . Does God give you the Spirit

so freely and work miracles among you because you
practice the Law, or because you believed what was
preached to you? [Galatians 3:1–5]

"Has someone put a spell on you?" The phrase is accurate.
The "spell" is the magical curse laid on by the Parent. As
we saw in the last chapter, a genuine conversion may still
be far from complete. The Parent may make a comeback,
especially if the whole language of the religious tradition
in which it happens is Parent-type language. The Jewish
tradition was not in itself "legalist," for in the true tradition the "Law" was not a set of rules and observances, but
the rules and observances were an expression, in every
aspect of daily life, of a people's dedication to God. One
has only to read the book of Isaiah, or the Psalms, to recognize the cry of genuine conversion. But the history of the
Jewish people for several generations before the time of
Jesus had helped to make them concentrate on observances. To maintain national self-respect under foreign
conquerors, the keeping of every detail of the Law was important in itself. It proved they were "different" from the
Gentiles, they were the chosen ones, however powerful
and rich and educated their pagan neighbors might be.
This is the protective Parent, strong and rigid and comforting. But that confidence had been undermined, all the
same, and the people were ready for another message. And
when the message reached them, in spite of the powerful
voice of that Communal Parent, they discovered it was
often using words they had been hearing all their lives.

The same thing happens now, and the recent growth of
the "charismatic" movement in all churches makes particularly clear how the old words and actions can suddenly
display what has always been their "real" meaning,
though it took such a personal upheaval to make it apparent. One particularly good example of this is the effect of
such experience on some members of the famous Trapp
family. The story of their earlier lives, when they lived

"according to the Law," as Paul says, reveals how very satisfying and rich a human experience that can be when the "Law" is a good law. The book Maria von Trapp wrote tells the story of the escape from the Nazis and their phenomenal rise to fame as a "singing family," and the treacly sentimental film "The Sound of Music" made use of the family story (altered almost beyond recognition) to introduce the Trapps to an enormous audience. To many of those who saw it, the Trapp family became a symbol of Christian family life at its best. They were courageous, devoted, and devout, they trusted God and tried to do his will, and succeeded in bringing the Gospel message to many by their friendly, generous lives and simple faith. This faith was built on three things: the reading of Scripture; the keeping of the ancient feasts of the Church, with all the local custom and celebration of their Austrian culture; and prayer—mostly vocal prayer—asking and thanking. This is what Christian life means for most devout people, whatever Christian tradition they belong to, and the story told by Maria von Trapp shows the mixture at work, one Lent in the old house, before the Nazis came:

> Some time before Ash Wednesday my husband and I were figuring out what we should do together with the children during the Season of Lent.
> ". . . I wish that my children would get thoroughly acquainted with Holy Scripture. . . . Let's start them with the New Testament and let's read it together every evening until Easter. And I guess I'll give up smoking," he continued, and this grave announcement was followed by a sigh which seemed to come up from the depths of the earth, because he was a heavy smoker.
> Generosity calls for generosity.
> "Then I won't even look at candy or any pastry," said I, and my sigh wasn't a bit different, because mine is a sweet tooth.

"We shall leave it to the children to choose their own mortifications," said Georg; and it was interesting to see what followed. One saw the whole character in the making from the way each one reacted. . . .

It turned out to be a beautiful six weeks. The reading of the Gospels together proved to be wonderful. . . .

Then Holy Week was close at hand, with Palm Sunday ushering it in; we made little excursions into the woods and came home with armloads of pussy willows. With the help of small branches of boxwood and fir twigs they were arranged into nice, round bouquets, fastened to a stick about three feet long. From the workshop we got nice, curly wood shavings, which were dyed blue, red, and yellow with Easter-egg dye, and hung all over the bouquets. They looked lovely and cheerful, and on Palm Sunday the church was a sight. Hundreds of children, each one with his *Palmbuschn,* jealously rivaling his neighbor's in beauty. They were blessed in a special solemn way by the priest in remembrance of the palm branches which were used to make Christ's entrance into Jerusalem such a triumphant one.

The customs are probably of pagan origin, but mixed to form a Christian culture centuries old, and blended with stories of the life of Jesus and celebration of his act of redemption. They are accompanied by encouragement to personal self-discipline, and by the words of the Gospel—perhaps not well interpreted, for they are two thousand years old and translated through at least three languages. The customs, the rules, are not spontaneous personal expressions of faith and love, they are the teaching of the Communal Parent, passed on with more or less conscientiousness by generation after generation of parents and teachers and priests. They are the "morality" and "dogma" of Christian life, those things which many in search of "au-

thentic spirituality" condemn as "enslaving" and "dead."
Yet, when the time came, the Trapps faced ruin and exile
rather than give up this dogma, this morality.

"Children," and their father's voice did not sound
like his everyday one, "children, we have the choice
now: do we want to keep the material goods we still
have: this our home with the ancient furniture, our
friends, and all the things we are fond of?—then we
shall have to give up the spiritual goods: our faith and
our honour. We can't have both any more. We could
all make a lot of money now, but I doubt whether it
would make us happy. I'd rather see you poor but
honest. If we choose this, then we have to leave. Do
you agree?"

As one voice came the answer: "Yes, Father."

"Then, let's get out of here soon. You can't say no
three times to Hitler—it's getting dangerous."

"Yes, Father"? Giving in to the Parent? Or rather the
Communal Parent. Perhaps. And this pinpoints the difficulty, for the decision was clearly the right one, since cooperation with the Nazis—the only alternative—would
have entailed increasing moral and spiritual degradation.
So is it perhaps right to obey the Parent? Sometimes? And
what happens to conversion? The answer is that the right
kind of Parent decisions prepare the way for the liberation
of the Child, later, not because this is what the particular
Parent-voice in the individual wants, but because the tradition, the Communal Parent, was originally created by
fully converted people and expresses their insights about
what freedom requires.

Paul knew all about this and wrestled with the problems
it raises. There is an intriguing passage in his letter to the
Romans, in which he is struggling to express the baffling,
contradictory nature of human reactions to moral insights.
His "I," here, is his personal expression of the common

human lot: "The Law, of course, as we all know, is spiritual; but I am unspiritual; I have been sold as a slave to sin. I cannot understand my own behavior. I fail to carry out the things I want to do, and I find myself doing the very things I hate" (Rom. 7:14–15).

"Spiritual" for Paul, means liberated, autonomous, wholly open to God. The Law is spiritual, he says, yet in other places (to the Galatians, for instance) he says that "those who rely on keeping the Law are under a curse." The point is that the Law expresses man's liberated awareness of what his real needs and nature are when he is fully open to the Spirit who speaks in him. But the words that express it are limited by the limits of any human time, place, or culture. So those who "rely on keeping the Law" (as opposed to living it) are indeed under a curse, the familiar Parent curse. Yet, as Paul repeats, the Law is good, and holy. The "ego state" that recognizes the rightness of the Law is the Adult, but what usually enforces it, with interior sanctions of guilt and fear, is the Parent. But the Child, seeking freedom, rebels against the Parent, and so "I find myself (Child) doing the very things I (Adult) hate." The way forward is for the Adult to rethink the reasons for obedience and persuade the Child to accept them, if they make sense. This is not conversion, this is "being good," but it opens the way to real freedom, as with the old man Simeon, who was "an upright and devout man, he looked forward to Israel's comforting." So when the time came he recognized the Holy One even in the shape of a peasant baby.

But Paul still says that he is "sold as a slave to sin," which seems odd if in fact the Law is the road to freedom (the road, not the thing itself). He explains this in a previous passage. I have chosen the key sentences:

Sin entered the world through one man, and through sin death. . . . Sin existed in the world long before the Law was given. [This is true to individual experi-

ence. The small child knows "sin" long before he has
any notion of Parent morality.] There was no Law and
so no one could be accused of "law-breaking," yet
death reigned over all. . . .

When Law came, it was to multiply the opportunities
of falling, but however great the number of sins com-
mitted, grace was even greater; . . . Before our conversion our sinful passions, quite unsubdued by the
Law, fertilized our bodies to make them give birth to
death. But now we are rid of the Law, freed by death
from our imprisonment, free to serve in the new spiritual way and not the old way of the written law. Does
it follow that the Law itself is sin? Of course not. What
I mean is that I should not have known what sin was
except for the Law. [Rom. 5:12–14, 20; 7:5–7]

This is why "I have been sold as a slave to sin," by the
Parent injunctions. The unliberated Child (who is emotional, passionate, and capable of great evil as we saw in
the last chapter) constantly rebels against the Parent, by-
passing the Adult who is temporarily incapacitated by the
encounter between the two. Then "I find myself doing the
very things I hate": In time, if the Law is good and the
Adult sees that it is good, the Child is to some extent disciplined, and also comforted and helped by the pattern of
life created by a good Law. But this still is not conversion.
As Maria von Trapp said years later, in an interview, looking back on those days (and we must not forget the
courage and sheer goodness of such lives):

Before, we strove for perfection by the sweat of our
brow, and didn't get very far. Even in living a dedicated Christian life there can be something important
missing, the power of the Spirit. . . . We may even go
to daily Communion all our lives and yet never have
confronted the great issue of whether He is *my* Sa-
viour and Lord. . . . We need to consciously awaken

to Him and make a *personal* person-to-person commitment. I believe that one of the things the Holy Spirit
is doing in the charismatic renewal is lifting the veil
that has kept many Catholics from the personal relationship with Jesus that is there for the asking.

And not Catholics only. It is noticeable that the language used here is still the same familiar Christian language, though it has (as she herself noticed in another part
of the interview) a "protestant" tone in places. The "striving for perfection" is an Adult effort, though probably
egged on by the Parent. It achieves results, but not star-
tling ones. But it is, or rather it should be, a preparation for
conversion, as it was for her. Part of this preparation is the
awareness of moral standards.

The Law shows what is wrong, what to strive for, but it
is easy to feel that we would be much better off not knowing. As Paul himself said "Once, when there was no Law,
I was alive." We know the absorbed contentment of the
small child exploring his world, trying everything, before
Mother says "No! Don't touch!" Man longs for that Golden
Age of the Noble Savage—who actually never existed, as
Mircea Eliade points out: "The Good Savage praised by
Western travellers and theorists was continually pre-oc-
cupied by the 'origins,' by the initial events which had
made him, inasmuch as he was a 'fallen' being, destined to
death. . . ."

So Westerners idealized the Polynesian islanders, pro-
jecting onto them their dream of an innocent, amoral paradise, free from rules and so from guilt. The fact that the
islanders had many rules (different from the Western ones,
certainly) carefully adapted to their conditions, did not
shake this belief, nor did the Polynesian mothers' custom
of killing off unwanted babies by strangling.

We want to believe that only Law makes sin. Yet, as we
saw in the first chapter, sin is not a collection of evil acts
by guilty individuals: sin is the wrong direction, the wrong

use, of human nature, and it "invades" the child from the moment of birth or before, even though each new baby does come "trailing clouds of glory" and capable of Paradise. So however guiltless the "sinner" who puts his hand in the fire, it gets burned. Then wise mothers say to the exploring baby, "Don't touch it!" and put up fire guards. Or if they fail to, society rightly blames them. Fire burns, human flesh is vulnerable. And certain kinds of moral behavior also "burn," however unknowingly the "sinner" offends. So Mother says "Don't touch it," and puts a guard of regulations around the use of, say, sex, or property, to indicate which uses are beneficial (to the community, and in it to the individual) and which harmful. "Mother" may be Moses, or Church, or the Koran. All such Communal Mothers say "Don't touch it," though which things different Communal Mothers regard as safe ("You can have candy after dinner") or dangerous ("*Never* talk to strangers") naturally varies from one set of circumstances to another. The Law, in its manifold forms, defines what is required in order to live rightly, but it does not enable people to do so. In that sense, it makes things worse—yet only the strong sense that there is something wrong, and that it could be better, makes people grope and search for the real freedom. This is shown very strikingly in the account of work with addicts in New York, given by David Wilkerson in his book *Born Old*. The Center for young addicts and other "social rejects" accepted anyone who really wanted to get himself straightened out, but of course many did not persevere, at least the first time. A young married couple, apparently doing well in the little apartment allocated to them, finally grew resentful because one of the regulations of the Center forbade outings on public holidays. The reason for the rule was that contact with revelers, drunk or "high" and out on the streets, could easily be too much for the fragile resolution of new converts to "right doing," however sincere. The young couple told themselves this rule showed "lack of trust," and they disappeared on New Year's Eve, leaving their baby daughter alone. They went right back to their old haunts, were cheated by a pusher, then borrowed money and got everything they could buy. But it was not as good as in the past. At last the young wife came back, miserable and ashamed, and worried about the baby. "It's different when you know there's a right and wrong way to live," Anna said. "It just isn't fun to be wrong any more."

Another woman, still too embittered to give up her fantasies and come back, yet admitted to a worker from the Center: "It ain't the same as it used to be. I know better now, and I'm uncomfortable living like this."

The Law is "spiritual," because it prepares the way for the breakthrough of the Spirit, and also because it expresses the insights of the converted into the true needs of human nature. But also it enslaves, it is a curse, when it is used *not* as a way to God's love but as a substitute for it.

Here are some passages describing the way of life of two groups of men in religious communities, both dedicated to living the Christian life as completely as possible. The first describes the vocation of the Catholic Petits Frères, the "little brothers" who live in small groups in whatever apartment or house they can find in the poor quarters of cities. It is written by their Prior, René Voillaume:

> Our Lord has asked us to love men exactly as he loved them, and the Petits Frères' way of life might be summed up by saying that they must do their utmost to ensure that what they feel, what they do, and how they live, forms as perfect an expression as possible of our Lord's own feelings towards mankind. This mission is so absolute that everything must be subordinated to it. [Cited by Geoffrey Moorhouse in *Against All Reasons*]

And here are the words of Roger Schutz, founder and Prior of the Protestant Taizé community: "We must discover in our own field, in our place of work, the means of

radiating—perhaps without a word—the presence of
Christ." Thus, at his profession a Brother of Taizé must
promise, among other things, to "henceforth fulfill the service of God in our Community, in communion with your
Brothers," and also "renouncing all property," to "live
with your brothers not only in community of material
goods but also in community of spiritual goods, while
striving for openness of heart." [ibid.]

These two, Catholic and Protestant, are modern Christian communities, but they are both in the mainstream of
Christian community living, and their aims remind one
strongly of those of the earliest Christian commune, whose
members were "united heart and soul; no one claimed for
his own use anything that he had, as everything they
owned was held in common. The apostles continued to
testify to the resurrection of the Lord Jesus with great
power." St. Benedict, Father of monks, put the same notions into practice in his own time, creating the Western
monastic tradition. Its vitality and power to lead men to
God have been demonstrated over and over again, when it
seemed as though the whole tradition had died from the
sheer weight of its own worldliness and inertia. It always
revives, because the Rule, like those of Taizé or of the
Petits Frères, is the Law of love, expressed in terms of
daily living, by men fully freed by the Spirit. We can
sense, in the passages quoted, the wholehearted love of
the liberated Child, guided by the observant and realistic
Adult (who, naturally, is the one who *writes* a "Rule" or a
"Law"!) and appreciative of, but not cowed by, the legacy
of the Communal Parent. Yet such a Rule can become
what Paul calls a curse; it can become the stick wielded by
the Parent, to enslave and control, to enforce conformity
by bribes of Heaven and approval, or threats of Hell and
guilt feelings. The daily, hourly effort to make every action
express the Spirit of Christ can become the daily, hourly
effort to conform to a pattern of prescribed behavior. Here
are some passages from the massive *Usages of the Cister-*

cian Monks, as they were a few years ago. (Changes have since been made):

89. There are three different kinds of bows. The profound bow in which we incline until the hands are crossed on the knees, the moderate bow involving a sufficiently pronounced movement of the head and shoulders, and the slight bow which consists in bowing the head only. . . .

255. When we meet we salute each other with a moderate bow . . . it is proper that the junior salute the senior first. [Yet, Jesus said, "Anyone who wants to be great among you must be your servant."] In our relations with each other we avoid all unbecoming familiarity.

287. Monks, who are poor with the poor Christ, live by the labour of their hands. As soon as the signal for work is given, we go to the Auditorium where the Abbot assigns to each one his task. We tie up our robes modestly or put on work clothes—an apron, smock, or overalls, according to the nature of the work. We also change the shoes if necessary. . . .

228. . . . . If we complete the task before the end of work time, we go to the common work or the work room. . . .

290. He who presides may grant a period of rest about the middle of the time of work. . . .

294. If the Abbot considers it necessary, he may have the community prepare the vegetables during the Compline reading. . . .

What has happened to the desire to live Christ at every moment? It has become a series of regulations, all quite sensible but none of them necessary to thoughtful people who understand fully what they are doing. Do dedicated, normally intelligent people really need to be solemnly ordered to change their shoes before doing dirty work? Or to go and help someone else when their own job is done? Does it matter how one bows, and wouldn't a nice wide grin sometimes be more brotherly? And if special permission is required to get on with the vegetables while being read to, then the group of men must have reached a state of subservience to Parent and total banishment of Adult that does not encourage hopefulness about their capacity for full conversion.

Yet such regulations are made, in all good faith, in order to free people from petty decisions, so that they may have freedom to attend to God in the depth of themselves. And a good routine *is* liberating in just this way. The distortion comes when the regulation of every detail becomes an end in itself, and even brotherly love and commonsense are submerged in the passion for monastic regularity.

These passages refer to life in "religious communities" so called, but they show, in miniature, the tendency that endangers the generous, converted impulse of all religious groups, large or small, Catholic or Protestant, Christian or Buddhist or Hindu or Moslem. The Bhagavad Gita seldom refers to the failures; it conveys a vision of man rising to oneness with the All, above all human preoccupations, but in one passage the message of Krishna contrasts the genuine harmony of behavior springing from faith (the work of the liberated Child guided by the Adult) with the forced conformity of Parent-dominated religion:

Reverence for the Gods of Light, for the twice-born [what the Christian world calls "saints," or "the converted" or "saved"], for the teachers of the Spirit and for the wise; and also purity, righteousness, chastity and non-violence; this is the harmony of the body.

Words which give peace, words which are good and beautiful and true, and also the reading of sacred books: this is the harmony of words.

Quietness of mind, silence, self-harmony, loving-kindness and a pure heart: this is the harmony of the mind.

This threefold harmony is called pure when it is practised with supreme faith with no desire for a reward and with oneness of soul.

But false austerity, for the sake of reputation, honour and reverence, is impure. It belongs to Rajas ["impure mental energy and restless passion"] and is unstable and uncertain.

When self-control is self-torture, due to dullness of the mind, or when it aims at hurting another, then self-control is of darkness.

A gift is pure when it is given from the heart at the right time and at the right place, and when we expect nothing in return.

But when it is given expecting something in return, or for the sake of a future reward, or when it is given unwillingly, the gift is of Rajas, impure.

This passage forms an extremely acute commentary on those referring to Christian community life, for this Hindu idea of "harmony" is very close to the monastic ideal of "peace," both as a concept and in the ways it is attained. And the false peace also clearly has the same origins. And by way of illustration, let us remember the genuine faith and joy of the best Evangelical tradition as it was lived by such people as Adam Clarke, and contrast it with the same doctrine, interpreted without love, as the Bhagavad Gita puts it, "with the aim of hurting others," even though this aim be well concealed. Rudyard Kipling and his younger sister were sent home by their parents from India when he was six and she four, because India was held to be unhealthy for English children. They were put in charge of a woman who "took in children." Their parents were deeply attached to them, but they must have been very bad judges of character. In his autobiography, Kipling describes the household:

It was an establishment run with the full vigour of the Evangelical as revealed to the Woman. I had never

heard of Hell, so I was introduced to it in all its terrors—I and whatever luckless little slavey might be in
the house, whom severe rationing had led to steal
food. Once I saw the Woman beat such a girl who
picked up the kitchen poker and threatened retalia-
tion. Myself I was regularly beaten. The Woman had
an only son of twelve or thirteen as religious as she. I
was a real joy to him, for when his mother had finished with me for the day he (we slept in the same
room) took me on and roasted the other side.

If you cross-examine a child of seven or eight on his
day's doings (specially when he wants to go to sleep)
he will contradict himself very satisfactorily. If each
contradiction be set down as a lie and retailed at
breakfast, life is not easy. I have known a certain
amount of bullying, but this was calculated torture—
religious as well as scientific."

In his story version of that experience (called *Baa Baa
Black Sheep*), Kipling describes how the woman (Aunty
Rosa) and her son Harry tormented him:

> "Untrustworthy in one thing, untrustworthy in all,"
> said Aunty Rosa, and Harry felt that Black Sheep was
> delivered into his hands. He would wake him up in
> the night to ask him why he was such a liar.
> "I don't know," Punch would reply.
> "Then don't you think you ought to get up and pray
> to God for a new heart?"
> "Y—Yes."
> "Get out and pray, then!" And Punch would get out
> of bed with raging hate in his heart against all the
> world, seen and unseen."

The horrible thing about this story is that the language
used to justify this tormenting of a child by the "little Fascist" in the Woman and her odious son is the language of

joyous response to the God of Love. The "new heart" of
Harry's inquisitional method is that "new heart" of Scripture, the loving, open, liberated heart, set free from "the
bondage to sin and death" by the incredible message of
Christ's love. Yet here it is being used to *create* bondage
to sin and death.

Because of the terrible things done, especially to children, in the name of salvation, the reaction has been to
emphasize the mercy of God, which is a free gift and
which we can do nothing to deserve. Spontaneity, humble
acceptance of grace, childlike confidence in Christ's power
to save even the most worthless, if only they will trust
Him—this is an attractive proposition. It sounds so like the
attitude of genuine conversion. Surely this is the attitude
of the liberated Child! But it can easily be, simply, the
"good" Child, receiving comfort from the Parent, provided
he keeps the rules. The Lutheran Pastor Bonhoeffer who
died in a Nazi prison saw clearly where his church had
gone wrong, as the Catholic Church had earlier gone
wrong, though neither had actually altered the doctrine—
the "language of salvation." "Grace" means a free gift, and
neither the righteous Parent nor the sensible Adult can set
free the Child by hard work or good intentions. It comes
by a "word" from without, echoing within, and unlocking
the doors, like the "Open Sesame" of the story. But it
costs; it is hard for the Parent to give up and for the Child
to let go. The passage is very long, and I have condensed
it here from the chapter on "Costly Grace" in *The Cost of
Discipleship:*

Cheap grace is the grace we bestow on ourselves.

Cheap grace is the preaching of forgiveness without
requiring repentance. . . . grace without discipleship,
grace without the cross, grace without Jesus Christ,
living and incarnate. . . .

Costly grace is the gospel which must be *sought*
again and again, the gift which must be *asked* for.

. . . . It is costly because it condemns sin, and grace because it justifies the sinner.

This grace was certainly not self-[i.e., Parent] bestowed. It was the grace of Christ himself, now prevailing upon the disciple to leave all and follow him. . . . [as] he had received the grace which costs [i.e., leaving the protection of the Parent].

As Christianity spread, and the Church became more secularized, this realization of the costliness of grace gradually faded. The world was Christianized, and grace became its common property [Communal Parent possession]. It was to be had at low cost. Yet the Church of Rome did not altogether lose the earlier vision. It . . . was astute enough to find room for the monastic movement. . . . Here men still remembered that grace costs, that grace means following Christ. . . . By thus limiting the application of the commandments of Jesus to a restricted group of specialists, the Church evolved . . . a maximum and minimum standard of Christian obedience. . . . The fatal error of monasticism lay not so much in its rigorism (though even here there was a good deal of misunderstanding of the precise content of the will of Jesus) as in the extent to which it departed from genuine Christianity by setting up itself as the individual achievement of a select few, and so claiming a special merit of its own.

When the Reformation came, the providence of God raised Martin Luther to restore the gospel of pure, costly grace. . . . He was a monk. . . . Luther had left all to follow Christ [Parent orders?]. . . . [But] the monk's attempt to flee from the world turned out to be a subtle form of love for the world [The Parent comforting the obedient Child, conformity to Law out of fear, or hope of "reputation" as the Gita calls it]. . . . Luther laid hold upon grace. . . . He saw God in Christ stretching forth his hand to save. He grasped that hand in faith, believing that "after all, nothing we

can do is of any avail, however good a life we live."
. . . He obeyed the call, not through any merit of his
own, but simply through the grace of God. Luther did
not hear the word: "Of course you have sinned, but
now everything is forgiven, so you can stay as you are
and enjoy the consolations of forgiveness." [Parent approval and "stroking"!].
. . . The only way to follow Jesus was by living in
the world. . . . It is a duty laid on every Christian living in the world. . . . It was a hand-to-hand conflict
between the Christian and the world. ["The world,"
here and in St. Paul—and St. John, with a different
emphasis—means the huge Parent construct of customs and rules and relationships, held together as a
network of "game-playing" which keeps going because everyone is looking after everyone else just
enough to keep them going to play more games, satis-
factory to each.]

It is a fatal misunderstanding of Luther's action to
suppose that . . . it was the great discovery of the Reformation that God's forgiving grace automatically con-
ferred upon the world both righteousness and holiness
[The indulgent Parent!]. . . . It was costly, for, so far
from dispensing him from good works, it meant that
he must take the call to discipleship more seriously
than ever before. . . .

Yet the outcome of the Reformation was the victory,
not of Luther's perception of grace in all its purity and
costliness, but of the vigilant religious instinct of man
for the place where grace is to be obtained at the
cheapest price. [Looking for a more easy-going
Parent!] All that was needed was a subtle and almost
imperceptible change of emphasis. . . . The justification of the sinner in the world [liberation of the Child]
degenerated into the justification of sin and the world
[i.e., leaving the Child imprisoned but pampered, and
encouraged to "play games" provided they are ap-

proved religious games]. Costly grace was turned into
cheap grace without discipleship.

. . . . I can therefore cling to my bourgeois secular
existence . . . but with the added assurance that the
grace of God will cover me. . . . The upshot of it all is
that my only duty as a Christian is to leave the world
for an hour or so on a Sunday morning and go to
church to be assured that my sins are all forgiven. . . .
It is terrifying to realize what use can be made of a
genuine evangelical doctrine."

It is indeed. Bonhoeffer saw his fellow German Christians trooping off to church Sunday after Sunday while the
trains rattled by on their way to the death camps with the
latest roundup of Jews, gypsies, and other unwanted humans. Less spectacularly, but just as damnably, the religious establishments of our own time and country can
turn their backs on God's real demands, and therefore on
the real Jesus, while pretending to worship Him. In the
best-selling account of real-life conversion, *The Story of
Nicky Cruz*, the young evangelical preacher, himself converted from "drop-out" socity, is talking to another about
possibly using the big, beautiful city churches to shelter
God's most abandoned children. He gets this reminder
from the more realistic one:

Do you think those church people are going to turn
their beautiful buildings into dormitories for lost and
homeless kids? Those church people want to help, but
they want someone else to do it for them. They fuss
now if a drunk interrupts a worship service. Think
what they would say if they came to Church one Sunday morning and found their sacred temples dese-
crated with beds and cots and a bunch of former junkies and glue-sniffers in the spic-and-span halls. . . .
These people don't want to get their hands dirty.

It was this kind of hypocrisy which Jesus denounced in the professional religious people of his own time, and which, in our time, drove many who sincerely wanted spiritual freedom to look for it anywhere but in God, who had become the very symbol of comfortable selfishness and indifference to the sufferings of others. One of the attractions of Communism was that it offered genuine hope, founded in a coherent political philosophy, yet with that element of belief in the Golden Age to come which speaks to the Child's odd intimations of a Golden Age once possessed, or to be possessed "if only." It often provided no more than an "antiscript" for the young. This means rebelling against the Parent script while still being tied by it. To do that you just do the opposite of what the Parent orders: if the Parent lays down an irreligious, boozy, amoral script, encouraging exploitation of others ("Every man for himself," "You only live once"), then the teenager goes teetotal, goes to church, and displays a rigid moral code. If the Parent is the law-abiding, God-fearing, respectable type ("Honesty is the best policy," "What will the neighbors think?") then the rebel makes fun of religion, smokes hash, and wears his dirtiest clothes when the neighbors call. But he is still bound by the script, and Communism has provided an ideal temporary antiscript for many young people, most of whom end up finally on the commuter's train with a neat tie, short hair, and a briefcase. But some proceed to real conversion, or even start with one, and the reason is not far to seek if we accept Bonhoeffer's analysis of the malaise of respectable Western Christianity. Ignace Lepp, who later became a Christian, was an ardent Communist for many years, and his description of life with other young Communists, after he had broken with his family, shows why such a life attracted sincere people:

> Unless one has belonged to a cell of Young Communists, it is hard to have any idea of the intensity with

which the ideal of comradeship is translated into action. . . . When I became a Christian and started in-
voluntarily comparing either my seminary or the religious communities I had seen . . . with the Young
Communist cell, almost always, as far as concrete rea-
lities were concerned, the comparison went in favour
of the cell. It had altogether more simplicity, more
spontaneity. . . . I remember, for instance, a weekend
camp in a forest . . . someone let out the story of my
break with my family and the difficult time I was having. One of my comrades started a collection to help
me. . . . I felt insulted and humiliated, refused the
money, and fled into the wood. But . . . they had
been glad to give up whatever they could to help a
friend in need. . . . The district leader . . . took the
money and came to give it me himself. He showed me
how silly I had been to refuse the help of my *comrades* and made me heartily ashamed of myself for
having behaved "like a dirty little bourgeois." . . .
what brought tears to my eyes . . . was the wonderful,
instinctive delicacy of feeling. . . ."

Years later, after work as a militant in many countries,
often imprisoned, once sentenced to death for being a
Marxist, he settled in Russia. There his disillusionment
began. His description of the change in attitude is uncan-
nily like Bonhoeffer's description of the change in the
Catholic Church:

Ten years before, the Party militants . . . used to
boast of the changes for the better that had been made
in the workers' lives. . . . When they saw that we
were horrified by some spectacle of poverty . . . they
never failed to point out that the heads of government
shared the same conditions. Did not all Party members, factory hands and Commissars alike, draw the
same pay? . . . The situation was now very dif-

ferent. . . . There were probably no real working
men left among the Party members . . . the Party was
taking on more and more of the character of a . . .
forcing house for the political and technical leaders of
the Soviet Union. . . . Everyone talked contemptu-
ously of workers as peasants; . . . the moujiks, they
insisted, were lazy, ignorant and boorish—quite incapable of understanding the lofty aims of all the
plans for industrialization and collectivization.

That was the beginning of the end of a dream for Ignace
Lepp, as for many others who watched Stalin's Russia.
Newer versions of Communism have sometimes learned
from that, but the fact is that no ideology or religious system is proof against the "subtle change of emphasis" that
turns the language of the converted into the language of a
new game.

All such games, of course, are played in some combina-
tion of Parent-Child, since the Adult does not play
"games." ("Games," in the context of transactional analysis, means the way people exploit each other by saying [or
doing] things calculated to provoke a particular reaction
from Parent or Child, rather than to establish truth and understanding with the Adult.) This, regrettably, is one of the
reasons for the lack of success of some of the attempts to
find "alternatives" to the corruption and cynical materialism of capitalist culture. To listen to a meeting of student
protesters is to feel, often, that they (like so many young
Marxists) are using the philosophy of "ecstasy" or of Mar-
cuse not to express a real conversion (even a misguided
one), but simply as an antiscript. They are not truly seeking a new life or repenting of the old; they are merely
playing games with their parents. They generally use the
language of people genuinely converted to some vision of
an "alternative society," however, and the vision is definitely a religious one. Marxism is a religious phenomenon,
in that it provides an "eschatological" or "Golden Age"

dimension to satisfy the Natural Child, and a language with which the Adult can interpret and structure this vision. But the later "alternatives" are more clearly religious, because the myths and rituals that are a part of all genuine religious "language" are explicitly recognized, whereas in Marxism proper they are present but unacknowledged. The Child in everyone uses myth and ritual to express desires and hopes, and a good Communal Parent should encourage this. When it is denied—that is, forbidden by the Parent—it goes underground. When it shows itself, it does so as an "antiscript," of which Satanism is an obvious form. As the Black Mass makes explicit, it is simply an "inversion" of the Christian-type Parent script.

But even a Satanist is less dangerous than an apparently "straight" person whose "little Fascist" justifies itself with political or even "humanitarian" arguments. At least, with a Satanist you know what to expect. The existence of a "little Fascist" in many people, who are taught to disbelieve in his existence ("There's no such thing as the Devil!"), means that when it emerges it seizes on some form of Parent prejudice to justify itself—but the energy that drives it is the energy of the Demonic Child, as we saw in the previous chapter. This was the energy that created the heresy and witch hunts of the Middle Ages. (The witches and some heretics operated an "antiscripts," like modern Satanists.) Therefore, the newer forms of "alternative society" with explicit mythical and ritual content are to that extent healthier, even when they are misguided. And some of them are not, in essentials. There is an enormous variety, as this description of activity on just one college campus shows:

> If, on any weekday afternoon, you were to walk into a certain classroom . . . at five o'clock in the afternoon, you would find it darkened, the air pervaded by the cloyingly sweet smell of incense, and the sound of chanting coming from a group of hairy students of

both sexes sitting on the floor in the lotus position, rising only occasionally to sway in ecstatic dance. . . . From time to time the campus is visited by a singularly picturesque group of people, the Community for Krishna Consciousness, who dress in saffron-coloured robes, shave their heads (except for a single top-knot) . . . they make at least a few converts every quarter, who are then obliged to take up their distinctive way of life, a life of chanting Hare Krishna, living in total poverty in community, and abstaining from all meat, fish, eggs and dairy products. Or, if you were to be invited to another house on campus you would find its inhabitants living in what they call a Christian commune in which they say a form of office together, eat their meals in common, and practice various forms of mortification. . . . Again there is an enormous revival of interest in the occult on the campus: physics students who have scored in the upper percentiles . . . spend a certain amount of their time in astrological forecasting. Now some of these students are undoubtedly disturbed. Others, finding that wearing long hair is now grudgingly accepted by their parents . . . discover they can evoke wholly new forms of parental anxiety by shaving off their hair and putting on yellow robes. [This is the "antiscript" technique, as we saw earlier.] But the interest in, I almost said the "commitment" to, these and other forms of ritualistic behaviour, is very deep and very widespread . . . in practically every college and university across the land."

We should add to this collection the widespread drug culture, which is more than the escapism of the depressed or disenchanted "loser." Where LSD is used as part of a religion, such as that championed by Timothy Leary, the drug is used to create a new awareness of life and relationship, with the idea of afterwards re-creating "exterior" life in the light of the revelation. What is discovered in

"chemical ecstasy," as also in the enhanced state of consciousness created by prayer techniques, chants, and ritual
dance, is the consciousness of the Child, whose roots go
far deeper than individual experience. As we saw in the
chapter on conversion, the release of the conditioned,
adapted Child into freedom and joy is the turning point of
personal salvation or liberation. It is not enough by itself,
but without this nothing else happens. So this widespread
revival of interest in any and every means of "activating"
the Child is a sign of the Parent-ridden nature of our society. The reason for this state of affairs is the so-called scientific world view, a psychological result of early and one-
sided scientific development which outlawed all but physically verifiable facts. Feelings were "unreal" and could
be discounted. Prosperity and good health were to be the
foundation of the good life, and with that all myths, fantasies, and longings for other worlds or other modes of existence would vanish. Rationalism gives no scope to the
Child. The small person is a (possibly delightful) an-
achronism who will grow up all the faster if he is denied
such dubious entertainments as Santa Claus, fairy tales,
and, of course, religion. Shades of the prison house closed
in early, and even the view from the windows was blacked
out. The nostalgia for life beyond the walls was "escapism." As Tolkien says in his marvelous essay on fairy-
tales:

> I have claimed that Escape is one of the main func-
> tions of fairy-stories, and since I do not disapprove of
> them, it is plain I do not accept the tone of scorn or
> pity with which "Escape" is now often used. . . . In
> what the misusers are fond of calling Real Life, Es-
> cape is evidently as a rule very practical, and may
> even be heroic. In real life it is difficult to blame it,
> unless it fails. In [literary] criticism it would seem to
> be the worse the better it succeeds. Evidently we are
> faced by a misuse of words, and also by a confusion of

thought. Why should a man be scorned if, finding himself in prison, he tries to get out and go home? Or if,
when he cannot do so, he thinks and talks about other
topics than jailers and prison-walls? The world outside has not become less real because the prisoner
cannot see it. In using Escape in this way the critics
have chosen the wrong word, and, what is more, they
are confusing, not always by sincere error, the Escape
of the Prisoner with the Flight of the Deserter. . . .
Not only do they confound the escape of the prisoner
with the flight of the deserter, but they would seem to
prefer the acquiescence of the "quisling" to the resistance of the patriot.

Tolkien refers to two kinds of "escape"—the escape
proper and the imaginary escape, the talk and imagination
connected with escape and with "home." Thus, exiled
Jews longed to go back to a liberated Jerusalem, and some
have now done so, but meanwhile they sang, prayed,
hoped, and talked about it. "Next year in Jerusalem," they
intoned at each Passover feast. They celebrated their spiritual home, recalling and reaffirming its existence, and their
hope of one day being there. The evocation and celebration, in ritual and story, of the "homeland" is what a religious culture is about, and it is here that we suddenly realize why the young are searching so deeply for ritual and
myth, and also where we should look for a way to resolve
the problem evoked by Bonhoeffer and by those passages
I quoted to show the "fossilization" of a living religious
impulse. For Tolkien's escaped prisoner is the convert, the
truly liberated Child. He lives and expresses this recovered homeland, and bubbles over in a way that some find
ridiculous with the desire to tell others about it, to help
them find it, and as far as possible to make "Thy kingdom
come *on earth* as it is in Heaven." But there are also the
many prisoners who are still "inside." For them, the hope
of eventual escape (or better still of knocking down the

prison altogether) is the constant renewal of their certainty that freedom exists, that there is a world outside. To create and preserve this conviction, the repetition of stories about that world, and the enacting of its customs and relationships in ritual form, is absolutely necessary. Otherwise, even if the odd prisoner did escape, he would probably feel like going back to the familiar cells, because he would not know where to go, or how to speak the language. And this story-telling and enactment is the way religion provides *both* for the unconverted, to prepare their conversion and make them hopeful and happy meanwhile, and for the converted, to guide and develop their newly won freedom and teach them to extend it in themselves and for others.

It is here that we begin to glimpse the possibility of an end to the war between Parent and Child. For if a large part of the Parent content consists of injunctions and stories and rituals which are about the "free" world of the Spirit, then the Parent is preparing the way for the liberation of the Child, even unintentionally. The tribal rituals of initiation often include features which specifically symbolize the young man's liberation from his home and his mother. Paradoxically, we can now see that this would help the liberation of the Child in him, but this Child would thereafter develop under the guidance of the same rituals and stories and precepts that had been part of his culture from babyhood—only now taken on as a personal discovery and responsibility. This is how it should be. The danger of such a program becoming merely a "conditioning" is, however, present, because a very strongly ritualistic society can almost outlaw the Adult. Its members get along very well without him, in fact Adult comment and personal decision is only disruptive of a traditional tribal society whose stability and continuity depends on the unquestioning conformity of everyone to tribal codes and rituals. This works well enough, provided the exterior circumstances remain unchanged. But such societies cannot cope with change. This is why some Latin American tribal societies simply disintegrated under the impact of white civilization (even without the help of greedy land-grabbers and stupid missionaries). Since the Adult had been discouraged to the point of atrophy, there was no way to assimilate new conditions to the tribal culture, no way even to decide whether to assimilate, adapt, or reject. They tried to go on as they always had, and because the intruders made this impossible they lost heart and became apathetic, dully resentful, and despairing. It is not only "primitive" religions that make this mistake. The older, more "established" Christian churches have done so, and so have the great Eastern religions. Although the wistful Westerner sees only the surge and splendor of a great unworldly, mystical tradition, long lost by a stuffy and routine Christianity, the East can fall into the same pitfall. In the great evocation of Indian life, Kipling puts these words into the mouth of the Buddhist Lama, the saintly old man who, for Kipling, epitomized faith:

> For five—seven—eighteen—forty years it was in my mind that the old Law was not well followed; being overlaid, as thou knowest, with devildom, charms and idolatry. . . . [These are the signs of a genuine symbolic culture which has lost its "liberating" impulse through failure to adapt. The symbols become magic formulae, the stories mere tales, wistful but not personal.] . . . The books of my lamasery I read, and they were dried pith; and the later ritual with which we of the Reformed Law have cumbered ourselves— that, too, had no worth to these old eyes . . . it is all illusion.

So he set out to find the truth, and liberation from sin through the waters of the River of the Arrow, which flowed where the Lord Buddha shot it. In many faiths, water is the symbol of regeneration. In rejecting the accretions and the idolatry, he still kept the essential rituals and symbols and stories. And even the most radical Christian reformers, if they are wise, see the need for this. Those that have not seen it have usually lost their faith also, and they have certainly lost the hearts of the young who, their Child still unsuppressed, are seeking the place whence came their "clouds of glory." One member of a new, radical Christian group, living in the poorest quarter of a great city, told a journalist:

> It's the religious community that is most relevant to me, the one that mirrors most closely my concerns and my hopes. So many of us have become fed up with the impersonal, old-fashioned liturgy, the formalized blasphemy we have to sit through every Sunday for the sake of the Church . . ." [F. du Plessis Gray, *Divine Disobedience*]

But another one added later:

> There's a real danger . . . in secularising the Church as we have done, you can throw out the baby with the bath. I mean by that if you go too far with the Harvey Cox idea that picketing for better housing is a form of prayer, then you may end up with no meditative discipline whatever. The balance between meditative discipline and social action—that's the most important balance we have to strive for. [ibid.]

"Meditative discipline" means the careful Adult reflection on the Child's discoveries, and also on what it accepts or rejects from the Parent. That balance is upset by the type of religious group that concentrates on the inner experience, and rejects exterior action as irrelevant, as the dropout drug culture explicitly does. This is one reason why it did not grow as its followers confidently prophesied that it would. Their prophecies were based on their own interior conviction of the beauty and goodness of what they had discovered. Such prophecies were the articulation of "Child" enthusiasm, and bore no relation to the facts that the Adult could have assessed. The same applies to other "ecstatic" cults and sects, such as the Children of God mentioned in the previous chapter. Such sects can end up with a monstrous communal selfishness—the selfishness of the Child, wholly absorbed in his own sensations. It is here that the right kind of Communal Parent can help the Child to realize his own potentials. D. H. Lawrence was broken by his Child's inability to find a true development from his genuine experiences and seemed constantly to be thrown back into his Parent-Script (often the antiscript). But he was (perhaps because of this) extremely sensitive to the need of the Child for the right kind of guidance, and he saw it in the church, the Communal Parent, when it is also linked to that deeper and more fundamental Communal Parent, Mother Earth herself. The point is that the ritual of the church does not merely represent in myth and ceremony the events of the natural years, it also interprets them and places them as personal challenges and as part of the drama of salvation. Lawrence had no time for "meditative discipline" of the Christian kind, since all he knew of it from a Methodist background was negative, restrictive, and anti-life. (He clearly never discerned the original reason for such systems of abnegation—the desire to liberate the aspiring Child from irrelevant and distracting or corrupting influences.) So Lawrence did not realize how the seasonal cycle of feasts he described were fruitfully linked to the strong demand for personal commitment to the saving action of Christ. He saw the formative aspect of such a religious culture (Tolkien's prisoners *talking* and *hoping* about freedom), but not the wholeness of a life which had taken on, personally, the freedom that the great feasts symbolized:

The old Church knew that life is here our portion, to be lived, to be lived in fulfilment. The stern rule of Benedict, the wild flights of Francis of Assisi, these were coruscations in the steady heaven of the Church. The rhythm of life itself was preserved by the Church, hour by hour, day by day, season by season, year by year, epoch by epoch, down among the people, and the wild coruscations were accommodated to this permanent rhythm. [Lawrence seems not to have realized that the "coruscations" might be essential to the continued vitality of the rhythm.] We feel it, in the south, in the country, when we hear the jangle of the bells at dawn, at noon, at sunset, marking the hours with the sound of Mass or prayer. It is the rhythm of the daily sun. We feel it in the festivals, the processions, Christmas, the Three Kings, Easter, Pentecost, St. John's Day, All Saints, All Souls. This is the wheeling of the year, the movement of the sun through solstice and equinox, the coming of the seasons, the going of the seasons. And it is the inward rhythm of man and woman, too, the sadness of Lent, the delight of Easter, the wonder of Pentecost, the fires of St. John, the candles on the graves of All Souls, the lit-up tree of Christmas, all representing kindled rhythmic emotions in the souls of men and women. . . . Oh what a catastrophe for man when he cut himself off from the rhythm of the year, from his union with the sun and the earth. Oh, what a catastrophe, what a maiming of love when it was made a personal, merely personal feeling, taken away from the rising and setting of the sun, and cut off from the magic connection of the solstice and the equinox! That is what is the matter with us. We are bleeding at the roots, because we are cut off from the earth and sun and stars, and love is a grinning mockery, because, poor blossom, we plucked it from its stem on the tree of Life, and expected it to keep on blooming in our civilized vase on the table.

Lawrence was right, and the young Gupis, or Krishna devotees, or trippers, are showing us that he was right, by trying to re-establish links with the roots of their human nature, in the Child which we have so suppressed, or disturbed—or kept in a compartment labeled "Art" or "Religion" or "Sex" where it cannot interfere with the Parent preoccupations with money, "security," and "success." All the same, Lawrence only saw part of the picture. He, like the "primitive" religions, excluded the Adult. He lamented the loss of roots, but did not realize that without the Adult to prune and tend the tree of life, it cannot bear good fruit, however deep its roots. You have to want to make it grow, you have to long, not just for the rhythm and sanity of nature in your own life, but for what that means: the conscious love of God, understood, accepted, and acted upon, so that His kingdom may come "on earth as it is in heaven."

And that means death. It means opposing the powerful Parent, in oneself and in others, and bearing the loneliness of its withdrawal. It means the dangerous vulnerability of the Child unprotected by the nurturing Parent. Jesus died because the Parent in the rulers of his particular religious culture recognized in him the rebellious Child who threatened their kingdom. So they killed him. But they could not destroy the Child, and the early Christians knew better than we do when they made pictures of Christ as a beardless boy, a beautiful Child, the "Puer Aeternus" of mythology. Gerald Vann wrote that:

> . . . He should stand, for the Christians, not of course for a nostalgic yearning after a vanished youth, nor simply for an eternal recovery of youth, but again for something matter-of-fact . . . for the preservation, or

recovery, here and now, of certain qualities of mind
and soul which we associate with childhood, and
which are a part of the search for God. . . . St. John
tells us that "the Word was made flesh and dwelt
amongst us, and we saw his glory full of *grace* and
truth," and if we ask why . . . he should single out
these two, we may perhaps find an answer if we see
them . . . grace in the sense of graciousness and even
gracefulness, and truth in the sense of candour, sincerity, integrity . . . there is a candour and directness, a
sincerity and discernment and a hatred of humbug and
compromise, which again may easily fail to survive
the pressure of the "common day." We can never find
our true self if we persist in presenting to the world,
and to ourselves, a false self, we can never find God
unless we approach God with the simplicity and
directness of a child.

The "false self" is the Parent—even the good one. We
need it, as we have seen, to nurture and prepare, and ideally we might hope that there could be a happy transition
to autonomy when the time comes. As we have seen, this
can happen, but only at the expense of the Adult. And it is
the Adult, seeing clearly and honestly with Child eyes,
who has to recognize when the Parent is being oppressive,
or too rigid, or simply irrelevant—however good the
Parent-tradition may be (or have once been). So the Adult
has to decide, and to resist, and, if necessary, to die. Often,
one person is appointed to "activate" the Adult for many,
when his or her Adult sees, or the true Child tells him,
that surrender means corruption and spiritual death. Bonhoeffer, the Lutheran pastor, was one of these, and another
was the Austrian peasant Franz Jägerstetter, who died
rather than serve in the Nazi army, and so was the pretty
butcher's wife Margaret Clitheroe, who was pressed to
death during the first Elizabeth's reign. And there have
been many, in recent years, who preferred prison and dis-

grace to cooperation with government policies that exemplified all the Parent qualities of "paternalism," anti-intellectualism, vicious self-righteousness, dishonesty, and cowardly concern for the public "image" above all other considerations. T. S. Eliot provides us with a fitting conclusion to this chapter in his play on that theme, *Murder in the Cathedral.* The Chorus of the women of Canterbury express the world that Lawrence praised—earthy, important, bound to the seasons, to basic emotions and fear and hopes. They are in Tolkien's prison, not unhappy, but resigned, and aware that there is an outside world, even if they seem unlikely to reach it. Thomas, facing martyrdom, knows that this life can remain bearable if the hope of freedom is real, if there actually is a way out that can be found. The powers of the State, the oppressive, dishonest Parent (but in other circumstances it would be the Church that does this) work to shut that door forever, to make the prisoners' dream a mere illusion. Thomas knows that the possibility of freedom can only remain real in the hearts of men if, now and then, someone is prepared to die rather than submit. Thomas could have all the rewards of an obedient Child if he surrendered: he could care for his people in peace, and keep the favor of the king. But if he did that he would be caring for permanent prisoners. He would be their jailer, not their shepherd. The people, however, are not at all sure they want to be free:

We do not wish anything to happen.
Seven years we have lived quietly,
Succeeded in avoiding notice,
Living and partly living.

. . .

We have kept the feasts, heard the masses,
We have brewed beer and cyder,
Gathered wood against the winter,
Talked at the corner of the fire,

Talked at the corners of streets,
Talked not always in whispers,
Living and partly living.
We have seen births, deaths and marriages,
We have had various scandals,
We have been afflicted with taxes,
We have had laughter and gossip,

.   .   .

We have all had our private terrors,
Our particular shadows, our secret fears.
But now a great fear is upon us, a fear not of one but of
    many,
A fear like birth and death, when we see birth and
    death alone
In a void apart. We
Are afraid in a fear which we cannot know, which we
    cannot face, which none understands,
And our hearts are torn from us, our brains unskinned
    like the layers of an onion, ourselves are lost lost
In a final fear which none understands. O Thomas,
    Archbishop,
O Thomas our Lord, leave us and leave us be, in our
    humble and tarnished frame of existence, leave
    us; do not ask us
To stand to the doom on the house, the doom on the
    Archbishop, the doom on the world.

This passage is a marvelous description of that fear of
freedom which is man's great hindrance to salvation. The
old life, the prison life, is bearable, sometimes even good,
and there is the approval of the Parent who wrote the
script (Church, State, Mother, Party) to sweeten and comfort. The Second Tempter tries to persuade Thomas that
he would make a good jailer, that this is the best thing he
can do, to obey the Parent and act as his spokesman:

To set down the great, protect the poor,
Beneath the throne of God can man do more?
Disarm the ruffian, strengthen the laws,
Rule for the good of the better cause,
Dispensing justice make all even,
Is thrive on earth, and perhaps in heaven.
  THOMAS
What means?
  TEMPTER
 Real power
Is purchased at price of a certain submission.

And Thomas finally concludes:

Temporal power, to build a good world,
To keep order, as the world knows order.
. . . . Power with the King—
I *was* the King, his arm, his better reason.
But what was once exaltation
Would now be only mean descent.

This is because Thomas has discovered freedom. His Child, confident and joyful, is now guided by a shrewd, wise Adult whose language is that of the Christian Communal Parent, words of the Gospel, recognized as personal commands and distinct, verifiable principles for action. To go back to the prison, to the days of living by his Parent script, would indeed be a descent. Yet the Fourth Tempter, in a different way, always wants Thomas to surrender to the Parent, this time to a script laid down by the Church, the script of the holy martyr. This is so nearly the real thing that Thomas cannot understand at first that he is being tempted to "do the right deed for the wrong reason." To do so would be to continue to keep the people in prison, but one with ecclesiastical trimmings. But the liberated Child is honest, he does not play games with the

Parent because he is free of him. He loves and is loved,
and *that* is the reason why he will not surrender. So
Thomas goes on his way to death because he "has become
the instrument of God, who has lost his will in the will of
God, and who no longer desires anything for himself, not
even the glory of being a martyr."

Therefore, at the end of the play the women of Canterbury realize that Thomas, their Archbishop, has, by his
death, protected them from despair. He has preserved for
them the knowledge that, in spite of all that a Parent State
or a Parent Church may do, there is a real world, and even
such as they may reach it. Meanwhile, they can rejoice
that it exists. For the acts of the saints and martyrs become
part of the Communal Parent. The acts and words of Jesus,
the stories of those who followed him—these combine
with the seasonal cycles of the year's feasts and give them
a new meaning. Alone, the life of man is "scripted" by the
"rhythm of nature" and the rule of governments—Mother
Earth and Father State. They have no life to give, but they
come to life when the script is broken, when the cycle is
undone to reveal a door. When there seems little point in
it all and behaviorists compile statistics about the antics of
rats, and nice young men are trained to shoot old men and
little children and make a "body count," we need to remember that Jesus died to prove that God is the great
script-breaker. And when the name of Jesus is distorted,
and is used to reinforce the Parent and destroy the Gospel,
then there comes always another one to do what he did
and reassert the message of freedom. And the Adult hears
it afresh and is conscious of its truth:

Therefore man, whom Thou hast made to be conscious
        of Thee, must consciously praise Thee, in thought
        and in word and in deed.
Even with the hand to the broom, the back bent in
        laying the fire, the knee bent in cleaning the
        hearth, we, the scrubbers and sweepers of Canterbury,

The back bent under toil, the knee bent under sin, the
    hands to the face under fear, the head bent under
    grief,

Even in us the voices of seasons, the snuffle of winter,
    the song of spring, the drone of summer, the
    voices of beasts and birds, praise Thee.

We thank Thee for Thy mercies of blood, for Thy re-
    demption by blood. For the blood of Thy martyrs
    and saints

Shall enrich the earth, shall create the holy places.

For wherever a saint has dwelt, wherever a martyr has
    given his blood for the blood of Christ,

There is holy ground, and the sanctity shall not depart
    from it

Though armies trample over it, though sightseers come
    with guide-books looking over it; . . .

From such ground springs that which forever renews
    the earth

Though it is forever denied. Therefore, O God, we
    thank Thee Who hast given such blessing to Canter-
    bury.

4

Dreaming Dreams and Seeing Visions

TRANSACTIONAL analysis is a down-to-earth language of therapy—a way of saying what is wrong with people, and showing them how they can put it right. We have seen how this language can help us to understand the rights and wrongs of spiritual growth. We have seen how the infant, still "trailing clouds of glory" from his proper "homeland," is quickly imprisoned by the fears and hatreds and compromise of the grown-ups. A baby is not a saint, he is not the perfection of human life, but he *could* be, he has the "equipment" for it. Only he never gets the chance. Age upon age of adaptation to hard circumstances weigh on him, to tell him "No, the garden of Paradise is closed." Angels guard it with flaming swords, so the way back leads through fire. Returning means confronting the inner voice of the Parent, who has left Paradise and does not even believe it exists—even when he says it does.

All down those ages, men and women have confronted that fiery test and recovered Paradise, the "homeland" of the Child. They have known the joy and wonder of recognition: "This is where I belong, this is Home!" Thomas Merton says in *Seeds of Contemplation:*

> Although you had an entirely different notion of what it would be like . . . it turns out to be just what you seem to have known all along it ought to be. . . . We enter a region which we had never even suspected, and yet it is this new world which seems familiar and obvious. The old world of the senses is now the one that seems to us strange and remote and unbelievable.

But Merton is talking about what mystics call "contemplation"—the wordless, imageless awareness of God in the heart of the self—an awareness gained through long search and self-denial and longing. What has this to do with the sudden ecstasy of conversion, or the intense experience of all the senses which is reached by some who have the gift "naturally" and by others with the aid of drugs? Why does Merton talk of "the old world of the senses" as if the senses were to be discarded? Can he really be talking about the same thing? We need to be careful here. It becomes necessary to discover a little more closely just what is happening when a human being discovers that "normal" life is really a prison, a narrow, oppressive, artificial environment, and that he can and should break free.

We have seen that the conversion experience is, essentially, the "breaking of the script," by which the person assumes responsibility for his own life. He is able to do this because the Child in him, cowed and adapted by the Parent, is given the energy to claim his birthright. This cannot happen without help. Some "third party" has to intervene to liberate the Child from the Parent, though this "third" may be in the person's head in the form of a book read, a remark overheard, an idea suddenly remembered and recognized as important. This "third" one has to form an alliance with the Adult—that is, it has to present itself as forceful and relevant and strong enough to cope with the strong Parent. We saw this gradually happening in the case of Elizabeth Fry, and rapidly in the case of Paul. But it is hard. As Berne explains:

> When there is a [Parent] prohibition against doing something, a dialogue will result whenever that person starts to do it. The Parent becomes active and says "No," in a hard script, "Watch out!" in a threatening one, or "Why do you want to do that?" in a soft one.

These three forms of Parent can be verified from the three conversion accounts I used in Chapter Two—Paul's is the "hard script," with all the weight of Jewish chauvinism and pride behind it, Pascal's is the "threatening script," distrustful of emotion or anything not verifiable by reason, Elizabeth Fry's is the "soft one," suggesting doubts and loss of family support. Then, says Berne:

> The energy which the Child had mobilized to do it is then taken over by the Parent, and is used by him to restrain the Child. The more energy the Child had mobilized to put into it, the more energetic can the Parent become by appropriating this energy.

We saw this happen particularly strongly in the case of Paul, whose first reaction to a growing desire for freedom was to persecute the followers of Jesus—"breathing out threatening and slaughter," a typical Parent reaction. Berne goes on:

> Under these conditions, how can the Child be given permission to do something? If an outsider says "Let

him do it!" the Parent becomes alarmed, and his pro-
hibitions become even more energetic, so that the
Child alone does not stand a chance.

Here we see the need for that "third party," to act as
"script-breaker," by making a convincing contact with the
Adult. The Child can, sometimes, gain a temporary freedom. If an "outsider" can

> seduce the Child by supplying "energy" in the form
> of encouragement or pressure. The Child may then go
> ahead and do it. But after it is done the still active and
> energetic Parent moves in and causes the "hangover"
> phenomenon . . . guilt feelings, and manic-depres-
> sive depression following too much Child freedom.

We saw this happen, tragically, to Consuelo Sanchez,
whose Adult had never had a chance to develop, so that
her brief escape from prison was doomed. There was no
one to help her stay out, no one to advise, no map to follow. As Berne says:

> . . . . the Adult is the only force which can effectively
> intervene between the Parent and Child. . . . It ap-
> pears that the Adult can get permission from the out-
> side to mobilize its own energy or can be charged up
> from an outside source. [This could be a religious
> group or other strongly motivated community, as in
> the case of Ignace Lepp's Young Communists.] It is
> then in a position to intercede between Parent and
> Child. It takes on the Parent, thus leaving the Child
> free to go ahead. . . . Hence, the decisive factor in
> therapy is to hook the patient's Adult first.

So far so good. We have seen how vital the role of the
Adult is in guarding and developing the newfound free-

dom, but the Adult does not create the thing which is freed, his job is to understand its nature and needs—the "dogma" and "morality" of human life.

We saw in the last chapter how vital that Adult is in creating the kind of Communal Parent who will, in each generation, give the right kind of injunctions and tell the right kind of stories, and also of course encourage the growth of a competent Adult in each person. But all this does not answer the questions we raised at the beginning of this chapter: What kind of a thing is it that is released? What *is* this Child?—and after that: Is he the real Self?

It is important to remember that the Child is the "original" member of the cast. (He is potentially—though never actually, because Parent influences get to work at once, even before birth—innocent and *whole* and "sinless.") And there is reason to believe (according to Jung) that the Child has "layers" of awareness which link up with a *racial* "Child," with the myths and symbols of archaic man. At the level of *personal* consciousness, the Child's type of awareness does not differentiate between the senses. He has not yet learned—as he must to survive—to distinguish touch from sight and smell from hearing. Nor does he distinguish a sensation from its cause.

When life is going reasonably well, when a culture is generally pleased with itself (as ours was until recently), then the Parent recording will tend to provide an optimistic and positive view of life, varying with social status, of course. The Adult will observe that, by and large, the Parent sayings ("Work hard and you'll get on," "Be respectable," "Fold your clothes," "Say 'thank you,' " "The government will do something about it") are sensible though uninspiring. The Child's efforts at rebellion, in the teen years, will be tolerated by the self-confident Parent, and, sure enough, in his twenties Johnny will settle down to a decent job.

But when a culture is coming unstuck, as ours is, the Parent wisdom can look fairly silly. What is more, the

Adult will often find the whole situation too confusing and complex to work on effectively. With the Adult comparatively impotent, and the Parent guidance visibly irrelevant, the tendency of the Child to rebel is much stronger, and more likely to last. This happened at the breakup of the Roman Empire, then at the end of the Middle Ages, when the Church was "losing credibility," and again in the eighteenth century, when the "Enlightenment" left out too many areas of human experience, and so the Child went on the rampage in Evangelical or Romantic trappings. It is happening now to the whole of Western culture.

In this kind of situation, the Child in individuals and in a whole culture is disinclined to give in to the Parent's traditional wisdom. The Adult rejects the Parent but cannot provide real alternatives, so it offers little opposition to the efforts of the Child to look for happiness wherever available. It will even produce arguments in support. In this kind of climate, the search for ecstatic experience flourishes.

The study of "ecstatic" states might have been regarded a few years ago as an interesting sideline for anthropologists or alienists or hagiographers. Now, there is the drug culture among young people on the one hand, and the growth of the charismatic movement in the churches on the other, together with a smaller but influential following for many forms of meditation and transcendental experience by mental disciplines of various kinds. So this is no longer an academic question.

The search is not confined to such periods, of course. At any time and place there are specially gifted people (or, rather, people less deprived of original gifts than most of us) who can, somehow, return to or recapture the very deep Child type of awareness. Such people are mediums, mystics, and seers. They can often be aware of the minds of others or control the behavior of animals or insects. They "see visions and dream dreams." What they do with

these experiences is another matter. They may feel they
have known the presence of God himself. But such people
are rare. It would be fascinating to make a study of the
combinations of circumstances which produce them; at
present it is mostly guesswork. But it seems likely that,
with all the differences, such people are able to be, at
times, the "original" Child, with an undifferentiated experience, somehow still "in touch with" other creatures and
even other times and places. They can recover the awareness, and the powers, of the self which is somehow one
with the Self of God at the "moment" of *coming into being*
as an individual, yet still not cut off from the source of all
being.

It is not necessary to be specially gifted to have such experiences, as tribes that use hallucinogens ritually have
known for centuries. Drugs occurring in certain plants, or
manufactured synthetically, can produce similar experiences, as more and more young people discover. One characteristic that recurs among LSD users is a loss of differen-
tiation in sense experience, so that music is "seen" and
touch sensations "heard," personality "smelt" and dis-
tances "felt." Traces of this are found in language. We
speak of a "bright" orchestral sound, a "loud" color, a
"tender" heart, a "fragrant" memory. And there are rudi-
mentary signs of it in the way the tiny baby reacts to the
smell of his mother by turning his face to the breast, and,
when delighted by a pretty toy, by pushing his face forward to "eat" it. The kissing and caressing of lovers is a
faint survival of the association of taste and touch with
love and the Child's nostalgia for Paradise. This break-
down of the barriers between the senses is accompanied
by a removal of the "filters" with which the brain normally
suppresses sensations that distract the Adult from a particularly needed kind of knowledge of the nature of things,
practical knowledge that enables people to discriminate,
categorize, and handle exterior reality and relate to it for
the preservation and enhancement of life. Also, there is

often a sense of independence of the body, of control over matter and even of movement from one place to another, though the body remains motionless. Above all, everything seen, heard, and felt, and all emotions, reach an extraordinary pitch of intensity, whether they are pleasant (in which case the person feels he is "like God") or unpleasant, in which case there may be such terror and horror that the person becomes ill, at least for a time.

The connection, here, with the feelings of the Child is clear. The drug knocks out the Adult altogether, so that the usual way the brain adjusts impressions to verifiable effects and "objective" data does not interfere. The Parent may make an appearance, since Parent recordings start at birth, but it will be in a very strange form, like the magical appearance of witches and ogres in fairy tales. (This is because that is how the grown-up voices and deeds appear to the very small child—inexplicable, huge, strange, and often frightening.) External objects, too, appear distorted or unfamiliar, because there is no Adult to "tame" them, and the borderline between self and nonself is shadowy or nonexistent.

When the "trip" is over, consciousness returns to normal (unless a "bad trip" produces mental illness), but there is a memory of the experience, so that often the person's way of looking at things is changed and made more vivid. (Some artists seem to have something like LSD vision alongside perfectly normal perception.) But the sense of liberation, the awareness of having transcended normal limitations, has important effects, for the "trip" consciousness is so much stronger and more delightful (if it is delightful) than anything else in life that it naturally makes the rest seem dull, narrow, and futile. When the Adult comes back into action, it has this very strong impression to add to the normal "data" of consciousness, so it is not surprising if the experience easily changes people's lives. They have found a new world, and the rest can go hang. It probably will, according to some advocates of the drug cul-

ture, and confident prophecies about the imminent col-
lapse of the existing economy and culture, with everyone
"dropping out and turning on," seem reasonable enough
from that point of view.

The long-term results depend entirely on the "setting"
of the experience. Solitary experiment can be terrifying
and disastrous, and all advocates of LSD insist that a
"guide" is necessary. But if the "guide" is young and inex-
perienced, or older and concerned with being a messiah,
or if the whole group is disoriented and without a strong
"Adult," then the guidance can easily lead to further
"alienation" and rejection. Where the guidance is part of a
religion (old or new), it can make people's lives much happier—naturally, because the oppressive Parent is switched
off and its place taken by the guides or wise men of the
new community. But these sects are always of the "world-
rejecting" variety. They are there to cultivate the inner
world, not to improve the outer, which is unimportant and
unreal to them. Some explicitly deride the notion of
"doing good" as a betrayal of the inner vision. Contact
with the "outside" world is intended to bring others *"in."*
The philosophy is characteristically unrealistic about political and economic possibilities, yet it can, and does, make
people happy. This is because the Child is returned to the
original Paradise, and guarded there by the community
against ogres and dragons that might destroy it. It is a real
experience of the "original Child," and is therefore good.
In rare cases it can lead on to a more complete development, where the need for drugs no longer exists, as though
the person had been given a fresh start, a new birth. This
is what is desired and often claimed, but on the whole, if it
is a new birth, it does not seem to lead to a new life but to
a periodically renewed though blissful "Childhood."

But what is really happening is a vision of Paradise Lost,
not the entrance to Paradise Regained. It is paradisal experience that the ecstasy reproduces, whether one thinks of

it as a regression to the preverbal, pre-"adaptation" Child, or as mankind's "Golden Age" of innocence in the trances of shamans and other professional mystics.

The ecstasies produced by ritual initiations in various sects are different. There are so many versions that it would be unwise to generalize, but in most cases it seems that, again, the person is returned to the state of the original Child, but this time in order to be, in a sense, "re-Parented" and made into a different person—perhaps a god, or a representative of the god. (In some cases the shaman or mystic initiate has gone through a crisis having the character of a mental illness. This may well be because the Parent violently resists the attempt to wipe him out.) Afterwards the chosen person has special power of divination, or healing, and so on, and is "in touch" with the spirit world. This is common nowadays among oppressed minorities, who thus escape from the "slave" personality imposed by their Parent recording of humiliation and hopeless subservience. Some, at least, can receive this new birth, and thus give meaning and power to the lives of the whole group.

There may be a link here with that other version of the Child content, the one Eric Berne calls the "little Fascist." He is blindly and maliciously destructive and enjoys the destruction. We can see him at work even in the "innocent play" of the little child joyfully smashing a castle of bricks in Stevenson's *Child's Garden of Verses:*

> Great is the palace with pillar and wall
> A sort of a tower on top of it all,
> And steps coming down in an orderly way
> To where my toy vessels lie safe in the bay.
>
> Now I have done with it, down let it go!
> All in a moment the town is laid low.
> Block upon block lying scattered and free,
> What is there left of my town by the sea?

The exquisite pleasure of the torturer, the satisfaction of
the conqueror killing his enemies, the queer content of the
child pulling a flower to pieces—they are evidence of a
great energy animals do not have, the power to "take
apart" what has been made, and the sense of dominance
derived from this. The brick city that stood "in an orderly
way" is scattered and free—but free, possibly, to be re-
made into something else. The torturer unmakes his victim, reduces him to an object, and thus gains energy and
power in himself. The conqueror has unmade another nation, and added to his own, the destructive Child is asserting his power of creation and destruction. Siva, the pre-
server, the creative fertile power, is also Siva the
destroyer, whose consort is Kali, goddess of death. The
demonic, destructive energy of the Child is a necessary
counterpart to his creativity, for the kind of creation that is
specifically human involves the destruction of something
else. Silkworms work and spin and then die so that their
silk may make the robe of an empress. Trees were felled
so that Grinling Gibbons might carve wreaths of flowers
and fruits so light and delicate that they seem to tremble
in the breeze. Mountains were rent and plundered to
build Chartres Cathedral and the Parthenon. The spontaneous grace of a young body is restrained and drilled and
disciplined, and suddenly—the magic of *Les Sylphides*.

So also the perfection of human culture, the dearest of
human ties, must be destroyed before they can be reborn,
and the energy of the "little Fascist," when transformed
by surrender to a higher Self, becomes the energy of the
saint. He, seeing one great and desirable ALL, is prepared
to destroy everything in himself that stands in his way. For
the Buddhist, the body and all its sensations are barriers to
truth. They are the result of birth, and indeed we have
seen that this is so, as the newborn is assailed by the ne-
cessities of survival and the techniques for it developed by
his race and culture. Therefore the way to freedom is to be
detached from the senses and from all "worldly activity":

. . . . birth is the basis of all other misfortunes . . . for the birth of a body endowed with sense-organs leads of necessity to manifold ills. . . . The numerous afflictions of living beings, such as old age and so on, are unavoidably produced wherever there is Worldly Activity . . . and the mind which is dependent on the body involves us in such ills as grief, discontent, anger, fear, etc. . . . Therefore, once you have seen, my friend, that craving, etc. are the causes of the manifold ills which follow on birth, remove those causes . . . you must . . . come face to face with the holy, calm and fortunate Dharma, which through dispassion has turned away from craving. [*Buddhist Scriptures,* translated by E. Conze]

The Christian Gospel is less calmly reasonable in tone, partly because the Buddhist teaching is aimed at those already converted and determined to perfect that conversion, whereas Jesus, as St. Matthew reports him, is emphasizing the cost of conversion, the element of destruction. The sayings are well known:

You cannot be the slave of God and of money.
It is a narrow gate and a hard road that leads to life, and few find it.
Anyone who prefers father or mother to me is not worthy of me. . . . Anyone who finds his life will lose it; anyone who lives his life for my sake will find it. [Mt. 6:24; 7:14; 10:37, 39]

There are many more, and if we link them to the sayings about "spiritual childhood," we see clearly that the great struggle is to become free of the Parent. And a converted "little Fascist" energy is what can win this savage struggle.

In this struggle, ritual is used to "convert" the demonic Child power and free it for specified purposes. It seems

that ritual experiences—rhythm of hypnotic intensity, in-
cense, darkness, sometimes sexual activity, or in some
cases pain—can "knock out" the Adult by disorganizing
the sense impressions and powers of observation on which
it depends. In the absence of Adult control, the powerful
influence of the ritual words and symbols can make new
impressions in the Child, strong enough to "wipe off" or at
least drown out the original Parent ones. Whether the LSD
experience could be used in the same way I do not know,
but the trance of the initiate in an ecstatic sect appears to
be much deeper than, and of a different kind from, a hallu-
cinogenic "trip"—in fact the person appears to be unconscious of the outer world—whereas the "tripper" has rather a
heightened and altered consciousness of it. The similarity
lies in the way in which the Adult is knocked out and some
aspect of the original Child is released and reaches consciousness. A similar thing happens, quite normally, in
successful sexual experience. The ecstasy of sexual pleasure
equally knocks out the Parent (which is why it is useful as a
means of teenage rebellion) and also the Adult, who has
nothing to say about this. The Child is the sensuous,
creative, emotional member of the "cast," and sex is a Child
experience with the same advantages and the same limitations and the same need for "guidance" as the other kinds of
ecstasy. It is often included in the drug scene as well as in
some ecstatic rituals, for the same kinds of reasons, and its
links with the "little Fascist" are obvious.

The highly emotional conversions of revivalist or evangelical religion have been criticized because the reactions
are not "rational," and indeed when the experience wears
off there is often a rapid loss of "faith." But the whole
point of such an experience is to cause the person to "repent," that is, reject and get free of older patterns of behavior which have so far ruled one's life—in other words,
the Parent "script," or orders-for-life, including feelings of
guilt for Parent-forbidden behavior. The heightened emotions of the revival meeting, working on existing discon-

tents which are the Child's underground efforts to find freedom, once more leave the Adult with nothing much to work on, and the greater authority of the voice of the new preacher thus knocks out the old Parent without much difficulty. The Child responds to the offer of freedom and new life with an ecstasy of joy. The Adult is not entirely knocked out, this is not strictly an ecstatic state except perhaps very briefly, but it has the same character in that the essential ingredient is the release of the Child from the Parent (the old Adam).

The experiences of people in the Jesus movement show how great is the underground pressure of the bewildered and unsatisfied Child in our culture. Young people of this generation are, in fact, more than usually susceptible to "re-Parenting" of some kind, because the original Parent script is often indecisive and lacking in confidence, since the grown-ups themselves lack confidence in directing their children. The re-Parenting is like an "over-recording" on a tape blotting out the first one. It may wipe out the first entirely, as far as we can tell, but sometimes the two play together, which is very confusing. And sometimes the "second" Parent, though immediately effective, is not as strong as the original one, which was only temporarily disabled. What happens after re-Parenting of the "conversion" type depends, again, on the kind of guidance available. If there is none, or the original Parent is powerful, he will make a comeback and the person will look back to the conversion experience merely with vague nostalgia, or even with scorn, as to a moment of aberration.

If the Adult is strong, any outside guide may be less necessary, for the Adult can act decisively on the new knowledge and viewpoint. But in most cases the continuing support of a likeminded community with a good and consistent "life-style" is vital to perseverance. This can be seen very clearly in the case histories of converted junkies, in the popular books of David Wilkerson. The obvious difference between this experience and the other ecstatic ones already discussed is that it is, in a sense, "once for all." The new birth is intended to lead to a new growth and does not depend on the recurrence of the ecstatic state. It is explicitly intended to take effect in changing behavior and relationships, in a new community. The emphasis is more "outward," at least among the community. Though some "Jesus groups" are, in fact, very secretive and "world rejecting," they are not ecstatic sects, nor are members expected to have trances or be guided by perceptible voices or visions. The "Spirit" is "felt" in daily life, not in ecstasy.

The same thing applies to some meditation techniques, but these do not normally start with a bang. They aim at gradually "disconnecting" the conscious mind from its environment and withdrawing into a "region" where outward forms and ideas do not penetrate at all. This means that both the Parent (rules, opinions) and Adult (observation, reason, decision) are left outside, but there is generally no great climax of emotion. Because the journey is slow and gradual, it seems to lack the violent emotional joy of the suddenly liberated Child. On the contrary, although there may be accompanying emotions of joy and peace and sorrow for sin, etc., the main thing is the gradual discovery of a world beyond joy or sorrow, or rather a world where joy is so complete that it has no emotional repercussions. Some kinds of meditation seem to be no more than a way of achieving a peaceful and "whole" personality (no small thing, anyway), but others desire something greater. The real "mystical breakthrough" happens beyond the point where discipline and detachment have eliminated distractions. Is it still the recovery of the original Child? Possibly it goes "further back" or, if you like, "further in" than that, to the "point of insertion" where the individual is "attached" to God, at what some mystics called the "fine point of the soul." Although it is not essential or inevitable, in most cases and at some stages this process is accompanied by occasional ecstatic experiences or

by visions, and so on. This seems to show that what is
going on *is* linked to those ecstasies in which the Child is
obviously dominant. And here, too, the "setting" matters.
It matters whether these experiences are regarded as ways
to personal perfection and freedom, or ways to come to the
knowledge of God for his own sake or for the sake of
others who have still be "saved." The Buddha turned back
from the final freedom in order to show others the Way,
and many of the greatest mystics have explicitly said that
they were "sent back" to help the rest. Evelyn Underhill,
one of the greatest students of mysticism, felt that this
willingness to return to "the world" after reaching the
heights was, in fact, the perfection of the mystic vocation.
Those who remained on the heights were, in her view,
certainly great but less than perfect.

This element of communication of the divine has always
seemed important in Christian mysticism, and to some
Eastern types also. It is, however, one reason why some
Christians are extremely suspicious of another kind of ecstatic state, that associated with the "gift of tongues,"
prophecy, and so on. This is described in the New Testament, and most churches are content to leave it there,
feeling it was a special and peculiar gift, suited to the early
days of Christianity. However, it has recurred in small
sects at various times as well as in the lives of individual
holy people, in revivalist movements, and in the last century in the "classical" Pentecostal sects of evangelical
Protestantism. More recently, this "charismatic" type of
experience has spread rapidly in the older and larger
Christian churches, with astonishing results. The "gift of
tongues" means that after a person has been prayed over
by the group, he or she feels a deep urge to praise God out
loud, and does so not in the formal language but in "other"
tongues. This may be some unknown language, but more
often it is in "babbling" syllables, meaningless to the person uttering them and to those hearing them but carrying a
great sense of joyful openness to God, an ability to praise

with complete freedom. The lack of inhibition, the sense of relaxed and bubbling joy, the overflowing of love to God and to all those who are present, so that all are "caught up" in the Spirit—all this seems to show that here, also, we have an example of the release of the Child. The babbling speech may well be related to the preverbal sounds of a baby, who "communicates" only joy, not sense. The feeling of being "one" with the others present, and indeed with all whom one meets, is also typical of the original Child. The Parent, however religious, is set aside as irrelevant to this new and overwhelming experience, but the Adult is not "knocked out," for the person can control the gift. The "speaking" (and also singing) in tongues is not an uncontrollable force like the spirit-voices of the shaman or medium "possessed" by some other powerful "re-Parenting." It can be begun, and stopped, at will, at least after a little practice, and the person is entirely conscious and rational throughout, though filled with a joy beyond any normal pleasure.

Because this type of release of the Child is done with the cooperation and approval of the Adult, there is no "comedown." The first, overwhelming joy gradually changes to a more habitual sense of God's presence; the person becomes aware of a new sensitivity to spiritual things and also of a vulnerability that can, and usually does, bring great suffering. This, as all the mystics agree, is the price of continued growth in the Spirit. The reborn person goes on growing; he does not need to repeat the "receiving of the Spirit," though the gift of tongues continues as a "gift of prayer," keeping the person open to God and man. This is not mysticism in the proper sense, and the person who thus "receives the Spirit" may be very far from saintly, but it is a "rebirth" from which new growth can begin and, in some cases, mystical gifts may develop.

The development, again, depends a great deal on the doctrine of the group. In "classical" Pentecostal churches the gifts of the Spirit occupy a central place and are needed to assure the person (and the church) that he or she really has turned to God and become fully a Christian. For Catholics and other "traditional" Christians, the charismatic gifts are graces given "for the sake of the church"; they are needed and they are valued, but they are not a required proof of salvation. The danger with such ecstatic experience is that the experience itself will absorb the person's spiritual energy, and lead to a world-rejecting, narcissistic spirituality—as, indeed, some types of meditation philosophies do. Groups that expect and receive these gifts need to make explicit the Pauline teaching that such gifts are intended for the good of all, so that the Gospel may be preached more effectively, and the love of God poured out on his world without the hindrance of those doubts and inhibitions which are so common among modern Christians.

As a means of spiritual growth, charismatic gifts and mysticism are in a different class from other kinds of ecstasy. The psychological basis is the same, in that all depends on the liberation of the Child from the original Parent "scripting." But some ways of doing this seem to consist of a repetition of some Child experience, or re-entry into the original "Paradise" which does not necessarily lead to any change in the other areas of life. It may even discourage change, by making "normal" life seem empty and quite unimportant. This is not always so: as, we saw, the right kind of guide can sometimes use a "trip" to initiate real growth, as Aldous Huxley and other "initiates" did. But ecstatic sects which use deep trance to contact the spirit world stress in their doctrine the unreality of *this* time, and see ecstasy as entry into "original time" or Paradise, where the only true reality lies. The whole point of life, therefore, is to penetrate and inhabit the true reality. There is also a danger in those ecstatic states in which the Adult is wholly (or very nearly) "de-commissioned," that the re-Parenting produces a passive character, a person that will do whatever is suggested. This happens in "murder sects" such as the Mau Mau of Kenya. It can happen with immature personalities in "charismatic" sects, which is a reason for the suspicions some Christians harbor about this type of experience.

But the charismatic experience is in some sense a "rebirth," therefore the beginning of a whole life. And afterwards the gradual and disciplined and extremely arduous development of mystical prayer is (sometimes, but not necessarily) the way spiritual growth takes place. One of the encouraging signs connected with the charismatic movement is that people who become involved in it often begin to *want* to develop personal and private prayer. This links up the "new"-old gifts of the Spirit with the traditional development of contemplative prayer. This is not normally a sudden gift, though there have been cases where people seem to have "always" had it, but it seems likely that the release of the Child from Parent domination (however it happens) is necessary for contemplative prayer. What used to be known as "discursive meditation," on the other hand, is at first clearly a "Parent" activity, reinforcing the patterns of Parent scripting. Traditionally, this has to stop entirely before "contemplation" can be experienced, and probably happens when the increasing self-giving of the person (by humility, self-discipline, and strong desire for God) gradually weakens the Parent script, or at any rate the obstructive bits of it. At the same time, the Adult (reason, observation, decision) is used in this type of prayer, and is likely to expose aspects of Parent scripting that are not relevant or are a hindrance to the Gospel view of human life. The aspiring Child is encouraged, and often "consolations" and near-ecstatic joy show fairly clearly what is happening. Finally, the person cannot "meditate." (This kind of "meditation" has nothing to do with the technique of mental detachment from reason and the senses, referred to above, which can lead more directly to contemplative prayer. Again, this is not necessarily so, but it would take too long to explain why.) At this point, as I suggested, the person has reached "further in" than the usual "original Child" experience, and there is little that any psychological jargon can tell us about what goes on.

Since the various kinds of ecstatic states are connected with the liberation of the "original Child," there obviously is a basic resemblance between them. The links between the chemical changes that take place in the body (whether made deliberately as with LSD, or merely "accidentally" as with fasting, rhythmic music, etc.) and the spiritual changes are obscure, and much more research is needed. Which is the cause and which is effect? It seems that sometimes the chemical change leads to the spiritual experience, and sometimes it works the other way round, as in "conversion" experiences. (There are many similar ambiguities of cause and effect, as in the case of asthmatics who can get an attack either from some emotional crisis or from something to which the person is allergic, such as pollen.)

The big differences in nature and value depend mainly on what people do about the experience. All the great mystics have regarded ecstatic phenomena with varying degrees of suspicion, because these often involve silencing the Adult, leaving the Child unprotected against the wrong kind of re-Parenting, or even against a comeback by the original Parent.

The conversion experience is not yet enough; there still remains a long way to go. The "not O.K." Child still needs to be educated in freedom, cured of whining and of clinging and of malice. The Parent is still hanging around. He is no longer in charge, but he is still able to undermine the confidence and progress of the new life by unnerving doubts and destructive prejudices. He is still trying to get the Child to depend on his "stroking" to cheer him up in moments of despondency. *He is quite happy for the Child to have ecstatic experiences,* because as long as they are merely "experiences," they do not change the Parent control of the situation. The Parent may even encourage the Child to make much of these experiences, because when they wear off the Child is more than ever in need of comfort and reassurance, which the Parent can provide, in return for obedience to the script injunctions.

So the fatherly priest is quite happy for the good little nun to lie in bed and be ill and have visions of heaven; they only make her more dependent on his wise council. But if she objects to the lax behavior in her convent and says that God wants her to start a new one, with a stricter and more fervent discipline—then all the power of the oppressive Parent comes into play to suppress that initiative. It was like that with St. Teresa of Avila, who did not upset even the most rigid clerics of the Spanish Church as long as she was ill and docile. She could have visions, as long as they changed nothing. But when they transformed her personality, so that she seemed a new woman with new ideas (not so new, they were Jesus' idea), then all Hell broke loose. Vita Sackville-West described it like this:

> By implication she was attacking the whole rot and demoralization of the Spanish church, and the clergy knew it. . . . That she should put an end to the parties in the parlour, to the surreptitious notes passed through the gratings, to the little stocks of sweets in the cupboards, was of small account [these are the comforts the internal Parent allows the Child who is playing at being converted!]; that she should re-introduce the observance of true purity, true obedience, true poverty, and above all the enormous importance of God, was a great deal. . . . No woman lacking the determination, the inspiration, and the ability of St. Teresa could possibly have triumphed. This visionary was one of the most capable women the world has seen . . . the reader who chooses to pick his way

through the tangle recorded in the documents is left wondering not only at the dissensions and treacheries of the men of God but also at the stature of the woman steering among them. The venture raised an uproar in Avila, where it was said that Teresa was giving scandal and setting up novelties. . . . "There was some talk of putting Teresa in prison; and all the inhabitants, she says, were so excited that they talked of nothing else." And all this at the age of fifty-seven, after thirty years as a nun who had "inexplicable revelations of grace, but there was nothing unusual in all that, and a thousand parallel cases matched her own." But although she was "ravaged by the multiplicity of ailments from which she suffered, she entered suddenly upon a new stage of life."

Her conversion had reached fulfillment and issued in action, and there was no stopping her. No Parent-ruled clerics could do that, in fact the Parent in others gave way before her like melting butter:

She could talk round the General of the Order who had arrived full of hostility from Rome, but who ended by giving her everything she wanted. The Archbishop of Seville prevented her from kneeling to him and sank to his knees before her instead. Her own confessor was wont to say, "Good Lord, good Lord! I would rather argue with all the theologians in creation than with that woman."

That is the power of the liberated Child, when he has fully realized his autonomy, under the guidance of the enlightened, flexible, observant Adult, learning carefully and lovingly from the Communal Parent, not out of mindless subservience, but in thoughtful awareness of the divine reasons that may lie behind ancient and ill-understood formulas. But Teresa herself was well aware of how the Parent can trick even the liberated Child into niggling anxiety and fruitless efforts. She told the confessors of her nuns to make their directions both flexible and clear, so that the "tiresome" nuns would not fuss about whether to wear linen or woollen stockings. She also remarked tartly of two nuns given to visions, that if she had been around they would not have had so many extraordinary experiences.

It seems odd that beautiful and genuine "Child" experiences, desires, and hopes should be discouraged by one whose whole purpose was to liberate women from a petty, indulgent, yet tyrannical Parent and let them soar towards the great Eagle, Christ. Yet her emphasis on poverty, discipline, and distrust of "experiences" (even her own) is echoed by all the mystics of every faith, though some are willing to see the value of those moments of incomparable joy which show the soul that there *is* a world outside the prison. But they all know that escaping from the prison is hard and dangerous, and actually involves tearing oneself away from the view out of the window, in order to crawl through a dark tunnel under the walls.

The fact is, we cannot return to Paradise, personal or racial. Mircea Eliade, in his book *Myths, Dreams and Mysteries*, reminds us that the nostalgia for Paradise or the Golden Age, virtually universal in the "primitive" and pre-Christian religious vision, will no longer do. The shaman's intercourse with man's "natural Child" shows him able, as in Paradise, to communicate with animals, suspend the "laws" of time and space and transcend material limitations. He is in the "sacred" space and time, but must return to the "profane" sphere, which remains unchanged, without history or development:

At a certain moment profane time ceased to flow, and—by the simple fact that the ritual had commenced—liturgical, sacred time began. But in Judaism, and above all in Christianity, divinity had manifested itself in History. The Christ and his

contemporaries were part of History. Not of History
only, of course; but the Son of God, by his incarnation,
had accepted existence in History—even as the sa-
credness revealed in this or that object in the Cosmos
paradoxically accepted the innumerable conditions of
that object's existence. . . . In History, the separate-
ness of the sacred from the profane—so clear-cut in
pre-Christian times—is no longer obvious. All the
more is this the case, since for two centuries past the
fall of man into history has been precipitous. By the
"fall into history" we mean the modern man's having
become aware of his multiple "conditioning" by history, of which he is the victim. How a modern Christian might envy the good luck of the Hindu! For in the
Indian conception the man of *kali yoga* is *ipso facto*
fallen—that is, conditioned by the carnal life till the
occultation of the Spirit is almost total—and one must
go out of the flesh to recover spiritual freedom. [We
saw this earlier in the quotation from Buddhist scripture, which in this matter shares the Hindu philosophy of existence.] But the modern Christian feels that
he is fallen not only because of his carnal condition,
but also because of his historical condition. . . . For
we live in an epoch when one can no longer disen-
gage oneself from the wheels of History, unless by
some audacious act of evasion. [We have seen how
LSD is deliberately offered as such an evasion.] But
evasion is forbidden to the Christian. . . . Since the
Incarnation took place in History, since the Advent of
Christ marks the last and highest manifestation of the
sacred in the world—the Christian can save himself
only within the concrete, historical life, the life that is
lived by Christ. We know what we must expect: the
"fear and anguish," the "sweat like great drops of
blood," the "agony" and the "sadness unto death."

We have to go on, we have a history, and we have to
make it. And that is what the saints do. Conversion is not

enough, there has to be action to develop and express it
and preach it. That involves re-creating the whole person,
and that is not merely° an individual but a social undertak-
ing. It means re-discovering the Self which subsists in the
form of Parent, Adult, and Child, but which, for some reason, cannot grow unless the Child is set free first. The
Child is the creator, and the destroyer; he is where the
human personality is, as it were, "plugged in" to
God, but he is also where the Demon, the evil one, gets in,
for that primal, preverbal, psychic energy rises in evil
forms if denied its proper development. Therefore the
chaotic Child has to be disciplined, and denied; he has to
die, finally, so that the real Self may rise to new life. It is
not only the "father and mother" who have to be left to
follow Christ, not only the "great possessions" which have
to be sold and given to the poor, it is the very life, as we
know it, which has to be laid down, finally, in order to
"find it."

That is an odd phrase, when looked at dispassionately.
Why did Jesus say we needed to "find" life? And in contrast, why should we "lose" it, if we find it first? The life
that we find first is the "plastic" life scripted for us by the
Parent. It may be good and comfortable and useful but it is
not our own, so we must ask God, "Make me cocky and independent." Then, when the script is broken and the
Child realizes freedom, there is still the long search for the
Self which is in the Child, but is greater and deeper, and
much harder to find. As P. W. Martin points out in his mar-
.velous study of the search for freedom, *Experiment in
Depth,* even the liberated may be caught up again, if he is
not careful, in that *participation mystique* which is the
Jungian description of being scripted by the Parent (especially the Communal Parent). He describes first the
Parent-scripted person:

> People thus caught, so long as they remain caught, are
> incapable of individualism. As part of the mass they
> will be carried by the mass. If, as may happen, the

mass is quiescent, they pass pointless lives leading to
a pointless death. If . . . the mass is turbulent, they
will be hurled with it to strange heights and sudden
depths, following the archetypal way to glory or destruction of which they are not so much the agents as
the raw material. [We are reminded of Eliade's pre-
Christians, involved by ritual in the "sacred" but unable to shape the profane, which is "illusion."] Everyone, inevitably, is held by the *participation mystique*
to some extent. Those engaging in the experiment in
depth will repeatedly find themselves lapsing back
into a mass valuation, being enveloped by the collective atmosphere . . . and otherwise ceasing to be
themselves. . . . If the general feeling is blue, they
will be blue. If loin cloths are being worn, they will
be wearing loin cloths. If "a wave of indignation
sweeps the country," they will be found among the
sweepings. Or possibly they will consider themselves
highly original and say, wear, do, exactly the opposite
to everyone else—thinking thus to demonstrate their
individuality."

The last sentence refers, of course, to the fake freedom
of the "antiscript." Either way, participation mystique is
dangerous to freedom, especially when it calls itself loy-
alty to the Church, or patriotism, or family affection. And it
is still a danger to the genuinely converted, because the
liberated Child is still so vulnerable. That is why the mystics and saints insist over and over again that ecstatic experiences are not enough, and can even be a severe handi-
cap. That is why they insist on the long, hard path of
personal discipline, and also on the often unattractive duty
of loving people, not with a rush of joyful emotion but in
the slog of real work on their behalf. As the Bhagavad Gita
puts it:

The restless violence of the senses impetuously carries away the mind of men and wise men striving to-

wards perfection. But the soul that moves in the world
of the senses and yet keeps the senses in harmony,
free from attraction and aversion, finds rest in quietness.

There is no wisdom for a man without harmony, and
without harmony there is no contemplation.

Without contemplation there cannot be peace, and
without peace can there be joy?

For when the mind becomes bound to a passion of
the wandering senses, this passion carries away man's
wisdom, even as the wind drives a vessel on the
waves.

The man who therefore in recollection withdraws
his senses from the pleasures of sense, his is the
serene wisdom.

In the dark night of all beings awakes to light the
tranquil man. But what is day to others is night for the
sage who sees.

All the Christian mystics echo the insistent demand that
in order to find the Self man must enter into the "dark
night" or the "cloud of unknowing." It is the only way to
real freedom, as opposed to isolated "experiences" of freedom, wonderful and illuminating as these may be. The
natural, Paradisal Child has to "find" the life he thought
he already had! It is hard to admit one does not have it;
that is the reason for the immense appeal of religious or
philosophical ideas which say, in effect, "All you need do
is claim your birthright, you *are* free! Live as free men!"
and the concluding command: "Drop out! Tune in! Turn
on!" or alternatively, "Make the world serve men by
science!" But Christianity, often clumsily and tactlessly,
rejects these as a destructive half-truth. As Thomas Merton
wrote in *Conjectures of a Guilty Bystander:*

This false view tends to assert, at least implicitly, the
complete autonomy of the individual, who is no longer

responsible to anyone, who is . . . free to do exactly
as he pleases without rendering account to anyone
and without taking into consideration the moral and
physical consequences of any of his acts.

The Christian faith is the admission that one's claim
to autonomy is in fact rooted in despair and death.
While appearing to be an affirmation of life and hope,
it is actually a fallacious construction of the mind of
man, by which he hopes to create some kind of meaning in a life which will be resolved into the meaning-
lessness of death. The basic Christian faith is that he
who renounces his delusive, individual autonomy in
order to receive his true being and freedom in and by
Christ is "justified" by the mercy of God on the Cross
of Christ. His "sins are forgiven" insofar as the root of
guilt is torn up in the surrender which faith makes to
Christ.

But, as we saw earlier, this surrender must be the loving
surrender of the liberated Child to the Spirit which frees
him, not the slave surrender to the Parent.

It is necessary, for right and "whole" growth, that the
experience occur as part of an expected way in which to go
on growing. In this respect the charismatic gifts are especially valuable because they liberate "over-Parented" people, but do so in the context of a full Christian life, which
provides plenty for the Adult to work on, as well as providing a new "Parent" in the form of the ancient and tested
tradition of a Church with a worldwide mission. But the
Church, which, as Merton says, should be "the place in
which this surrender of individual autonomy becomes
real, guaranteed by the truth of Spirit and his love" easily
can become a "social mechanism for self-justification." It
can be a perfectly efficient machine for the manufacture of
self-complacency and "inner peace." That is why the
Church itself requires martyrs for its regeneration, men
and women who affirm, by blood if necessary, that not the

State nor the Church nor even the godlike, exultant, autonomous Child is Lord, but that only Christ is Lord. Because of the materialism and corruption of Western Christianity, it was necessary that men seeking freedom should turn to the East. The West had forgotten or killed its own prophets and mystics, and so the young reached out in longing to the East to recover the vision of wholeness and peace. Insofar as the Eastern teachings show the way to inner freedom and the Self, as we have seen they do, this was the right, perhaps the only way. But there still remains, for both East and West, the fact of history, and it will not go away. Once man has tasted freedom he has to share it and build on it or it is, in the end, mere illusion. And death is its end. And Jesus is the man with a history. Can he help?

5

Christ Is Lord

S O far, the use of aspects of transactional analysis has helped in clarifying the meaning of the fall of man, of sin, of repentance, and of salvation, as well as the meaning of words like "conversion" and "freedom." The name of Jesus Christ has naturally been mentioned frequently in connection with all these, but we have also seen "conversion" happening in contexts in which he does not appear at all. So what has he to do with it? Is Jesus essential or is he just a kind of symbol of liberation, one among many? Mircea Eliade suggested a more fundamental role for him, because Christianity involves awareness of the historical and therefore social nature of salvation, as we experience ourselves. Jesus is not just a symbol, he is also an example of it; in fact, as Paul says, he is the unique example, and one to be imitated. "The first-born among many brethren," Paul calls him, meaning that where he led we can follow.

If the language of transactional analysis is accurate, we would expect such a leader to show us what the liberated

Child is like when he goes on from his moment of liberation to discover the wholeness of the real Self. This self
knows no barriers and can therefore communicate fully
with others at levels of existence where even the wise
Adult cannot go, where in fact the Adult is no longer
needed, having done his job of education. And this process is exactly what we *do* find in Jesus, as the evangelists
record his personality and his teaching and his impact on
others.

This process begins before his birth. The strange an-
nouncements and prophecies about his birth, whatever
their weight as historical records, all testify to what the
first Christians thought Jesus was doing by being born. His
birth was a coming into the human, historical world of a
person whose freedom was guaranteed by the very freedom of God—"She has conceived what is in her by the
Holy Spirit," Joseph was told when he wondered how his
wife came to be pregnant though he had not had intercourse with her. "The Holy Spirit will come upon you,"
Mary herself was told by the Messenger, "and the power
of the Most High will cover you with its shadow. And so
the child will be holy and will be called the Son of God."
That "shadow" was the same as the "cloud" which hung
over the Ark of the Covenant, and filled the newly built
Temple, always the sign of God's special presence in
power with his people. It goes with the "glory" of God
which later the disciples saw on the mountain with Jesus.
The phrases are all images taken from the lightning and
clouds of a great storm. In Exodus, the cloud covered the
mountain, and the glory of Yahweh settled on the mountain of Sinai. The terrible power of a storm that can crack
mountains, flood valleys, and burn crops is a fitting reminder of the kind of thing God's Spirit can do in men's
lives, and it is out of this "glory" and this "cloud" that the
chosen Child is conceived. There are many ways to understand this; it could be merely symbolic of Everyman's
power of spiritual rebirth, and indeed it does have that

meaning among others. But when we move out of the realm of symbolism and pick up the bits of historical evidence the evangelists offer, we find that Jesus is not just a symbol.

The Jewish boy was regarded as a man, responsible for obeying the Law, upon reaching the age of twelve. But the imprinting of the Communal Parent was heavy on Jewish children, all the more so in a situation of persecution and political powerlessness. To honor and obey one's parents was one of the major commandments of the Law, and children were judged by society according to their conformity to this law. So if a Jewish son did disobey and upset his parents, one would expect this to be due to an outbreak of "anti-script," accompanied, naturally, by defiance and angry self-justification. Jesus went up to Jerusalem with his parents for his first "grown-up" Passover and took the opportunity to leave his family and join a group of young men who gathered round the teachers in the Temple, hearing and discussing the Law and the Prophets. He did not tell his parents where he was going, and they spent nearly three days searching for him. When they finally found him, they were naturally reproachful. How could he do such a thing to them?

One might expect slightly self-righteous, defensive explanations of God's prior claims, or else an inspiring assertion of the right to "be oneself." But the reply was neither defensive nor indignant. He did not play any games at all; he was only rather surprised that they had not understood. "Why were you looking for me?" he asked them, loving and puzzled. "Didn't you know that I must be busy with my Father's affairs?" He assumed that they, too, were as free as himself. His Child realized its intimate relation to the Father of all, the very life of man, and there simply were no Parent imprints to harass or upset it. But his Adult was still only partly developed—he did not understand the limits of his parents' understanding, because he measured them by his own inner awareness of freedom. So he went home with them and "lived under their authority," since he still had much to learn. This submission to their authority was part of the loving surrender to the Father which had also allowed him to leave them when it was necessary. He did not need to reject them in order to be free. He went on learning from and with them. "And Jesus increased in wisdom, . . ." for wisdom is the virtue of the Adult when it operates in loving partnership with the liberated Child.

The same realization of the possibility of an "unadapted" Child, newborn of the Father, is clear in the Baptist's announcement of the coming Christ. He warns those who come to him not to think that they will be saved from "the wrath to come" by saying "We have Abraham for our Father!" The Communal Parent (though Abraham himself was a "man of faith," as Paul emphasized) cannot save. "I tell you, God can raise children for Abraham from these stones," which is as much as to say, stones would be equally good. And, realizing this, the crowds came to be baptized as a sign of repentance, but John tells them, "The one who follows me . . . will baptize with the Holy Spirit and with Fire." When he saw Jesus he told the bystanders, "Look, there is the Lamb of God that takes away the sin of the world. . . . [he] is the one who is going to baptize with the Holy Spirit." And when Jesus himself came with the rest to be baptized, John protested "It is I who need baptism from you!"

John, a converted, free man if ever there was one, recognized one who did not need to repent. On the contrary, he was, somehow, the power that could take away the sins of others. As the sacrificial Lamb symbolized God's will to take away the sins of his people, so Jesus could really do it. Jesus, noticeably, called others to repentance but never even hinted at a need for repentance in himself, nor suggested that he had ever done so. This might have been merely proof of a monstrous arrogance, but arrogance does not issue in such gentleness, such deep compassion for the

poor and sad and sick and sinful. Arrogant virtue rejects
sinners as revolting. Jesus called them to him as friends. If
Jesus did not repent, it was because he did not need to,
not only because he had done no wrong, but in the deeper
sense that he did not need to reject any part of himself. He
had no "script" to be freed from, though he did have the
Parent as it can sometimes be for others also—a cherished
record of loving words and actions, mysterious and mean-
ingful stories of his nation, and all the customs and poems
and prayers of God's people. Somehow, the other Parent
impressions, the imprisoning "script" ones, did not "take."
Was it because, as symbolized by the Catholic doctrine of
his mother's sinlessness through "retroactive" salvation
(the "Immaculate Conception," which is usually confused
with her virginity) he had a "nurturing Parent" and no
"oppressive" one? Or was it rather—or also—something in
himself that did not "receive" the deadly imprints except
as something for the Adult to work on? He did have a
"Child" recording of reactions to the normal childhood experiences, good and bad. He was, later, agonizingly afraid
of death and pain, in a way that suggests some vivid and
powerful early impression. (He might, for instance, during
his early childhood have seen some of the rebels whom
the Romans crucified beside public roads as "examples" to
the rest.) There is also evidence of a strong inner struggle
in some of the accounts of healing, as if he had to overcome a resistance in himself as well as in the patient. Mark
reports that he "sighed" (some translations say "groaned")
when he cured a deaf and dumb man and went through a
kind of ritual to effect the cure, very unlike his usual in-
stantaneous healing by touch or word. The cure of a blind
man was also done in stages, on two occasions. The cures
which seem to have caused him some difficulty, those ac-
complished only with "sighs" and in gradual stages, were
those undertaken when the popular enthusiasm of the
early days was waning and opposition to his mission was
becoming more outspoken and fierce among the "scribes

and Pharisees," that is, the official "religious" people who
embodied the Law. It may be that we have here the traces
of a felt resistance to "scripting," which was harder when
criticism from people he had been taught to respect was
weakening his confidence in his mission. But there is
never any sign of "scripty" language or behavior.

There is curious confirmation of the absence of any
script in the stories of the "temptation" of Jesus. Whatever
interpretation we put on the nature of Jesus' experience in
the wilderness, after his baptism, it is clear that the
suggestions put to him were in "scripty" form. They assumed that he had some kind of "Messiah" script, and that
he would behave in accordance with ancient expectations
of the proper procedure for the "Son of God" who would
save his people. Whether we think of the tempting voice
as interior or exterior (and the two are by no means incompatible, in spiritual experiences), they seem to show,
again, that a script apparatus had been "prepared" for
Jesus but had never "taken." He recognized the script immediately, and evidently it had a strong appeal, if he could
later describe it as a real "temptation of the Devil." Perhaps it was at this moment that he decisively rejected the
script, which he may have been aware of, as an option, but
this was not a "script-breaking" occasion or "conversion."
There is no sign of earlier scripty reactions, as I suggested,
and his reply to John's reluctance to baptize him shows
this clearly. According to a "Messiah script," he should
never have presented himself for baptism. *He* should have
been baptizing, as John suggested. But, unlike scripted
people, Jesus was not utterly sure what was required of
him. He came to be baptized because it seemed the right
thing to do. (It is fitting that we should, in this way, do all
that righteousness demands, he told John.) It was, as far as
he could see, part of God's plan for the whole people, with
whom he identified himself. But he did not reject John's
notion that there was something a bit anachronistic about
the situation. He knew he was "different," but did not yet

know exactly what that meant. He was definitely not following a pre-set career of Messiahship.

The script, of course, is what the Evil One was counting
on. He can cope with a Messiah; he has met them before.
His suggestions to Jesus were quite predictable. Provide
food in the wilderness, like Moses: be spectacularly saved
from death, like Daniel or the Three Children in the Fiery
Furnace. Conquer the world for the Lord! The last notion
has a condition attached—"If you fall at my feet and worship me." That is, if you conform to the glorious winning
script I offer you. For the script is *the* means of preventing
God's real work. A scripted Messiah is the Devil's greatest
achievement, and the world has suffered from many—
Alexander, Frederick "Stupor Mundi," the bloodstained
"Messiah of Munster," whose reign ended in a crescendo
of senseless slaughter, though never on the scale achieved
by his greatest successor, Adolf Hitler. These and many
others less destructive and less grandiose were what Jesus
was refusing to be. "You must worship the Lord your God,
and serve him alone," he said, quoting Scripture. To worship and serve God means to abandon the safety of a
script. God is the script-breaker, and Jesus was able to
carry out his mission because he never had one, but knew
all about it. "For it is not as if we had a high priest who
was incapable of feeling our weaknesses with us; but we
have one who has been tempted in every way that we are,
though he is without sin," says the writer of the Letter to
the Hebrews. Without *sin*—never enslaved by the oppressive Parent, never self-imprisoned, yet voluntarily sharing
the imprisonment, he carried his clouds of glory through
life, and "we saw it," as John says.

From the moment of his baptism and temptation, Jesus
set out to discover, by doing it, what his Father's will was.
In a world populated by scripted people, his freedom attracted some and repelled others. The thing that drew
some to him like a magnet was his power to break scripts.
He called it healing, and he healed illnesses of body,

mind, and spirit as a matter of course, claiming this as a
natural result of being the one God had sent to set men
free. (But at times he was driven to tell the healed not to
chatter about it, because everyone was insisting on in-
terpreting his cures as part of a Messiah script!) He mostly
attracted the poor, the sinful, and the outcast. They had
"losing" scripts and were more willing to get rid of them,
whereas the prosperous and virtuous, the "winners," were
not too anxious to be set free.

He had a ruthless way with scripts. For one thing, he
refused to play games. This was one of the things that
made him most unpopular, for he not only would not play,
he was always breaking up the elaborate games other people tried to play with him. When the scribes and Pharisees
asked him for a "sign" that he was the Christ, they wanted
him to perform a miracle, for they could then either ap-
plaud it and graciously accept him as "one of us" or else
reject it as fraudulent. He first told them it was wrong to
want a sign, and then gave them "the sign of Jonah," out of
Scripture, a reference they did not understand and which
left them with nothing to say. The disciples, refused lodg-
ing in a Samaritan village, wanted to play Elijah and call
down divine fire on the impious villagers and have them
groveling to the Christ. They expected Jesus to join in the
game, but he just told them destruction was not his business and tamely went on somewhere else. The authorities
tried the familiar game of "Heads I win, tails you lose"
over the business of paying taxes to Rome. If he said "pay
them," he was not a good Jew; if he said "don't pay," he
was breaking the Roman law and could be denounced:

> They sent their disciples to him, . . . to say, "Master,
> we know that you are an honest man and teach the
> way of God in an honest way, and that you are not
> afraid of anyone, because a man's rank means nothing
> to you. Tell us your opinion, then. Is it permissible to

pay taxes to Caesar or not?" But Jesus was aware of
their malice and replied, ". . . Let me see the money
you pay the tax with." They handed him a denarius,
and he said, "Whose head is this? Whose name?"
"Caesar's" they replied. He then said to them, "Very
well, give back to Caesar what belongs to Caesar—and
to God what belongs to God." [Mt. 22:16–21]

The evangelist comments, "This reply took them by surprise, and they left him alone and went away." It must
have been very irritating for them, and even shaming, as
on the occasion when they tried to involve him in a game
of "Ain't it awful" about a woman caught in the act of adul-
tery. All he would say was that if they wanted to punish
her then the person to do it must obviously be one who
had not done the same thing himself. After that he sat and
made patterns in the dust with his finger, quite uninter-
ested, while they slunk away one by one. And the
wretched woman, left alone with Jesus, no doubt expected
exhortations to repentance and descriptions of the dire
consequences of sin. Here, too, Jesus did the unexpected.
He did what Berne calls giving "permission" to break the
script. "Has no one condemned you?" he asked her. "No
one, sir," she replied, answering Adult to an Adult question, probably for the first time in the whole affair. "Neither do I condemn you," said Jesus. "Go away and sin no
more." He knew she could break out of the adultery-script,
whereas her prosecutors took it for granted that she could
not.
   He also showed other people how to avoid games. The
recommendation to "take the lowest place" at a feast is a
command to avoid playing "I'm the biggest," a game to
which his own disciples were addicted. He broke that one
up by grabbing a toddler (probably a very grubby one)
who was playing around in the house and telling the disciples that if they wanted to be great in his Kingdom they

had to become "like this little child," which was not only a profound lesson in the nature of conversion but an effective stopper to the game being played.

In one curious incident we do see Jesus play a kind of game, but there is something strange about it, because it is clear that both he and the other player were actually pretending to play the game rather than being "in" it. It is an occasion when Jesus was seemingly uncertain of what he should do but was aware of a script direction in the background, as he had been at his temptation. So he used a "pretend" game technique to try to elicit the solution to his real problem, and he got it. It happened after he had crossed the border out of Galilee into the territory of Tyre and Sidon to get away from his enemies for a while. A pagan woman ran after him in the street, begging him to heal her daughter, who was "tormented by a devil." The woman, like everyone else, was assuming a Messiah script in Jesus. "Son of David," she called him, using a Messianic title. She was the suppliant speaking to the Lord, the Child to the Parent. Jesus did not answer at all, though she went on shouting. This was not like Jesus. He usually either helped people at once or sent them away if they were too antagonistic to be helped, or else talked to them in order to help break down the sickness-script. For him to do nothing at all was unusual, as the disciples showed when they urged him to act. "Give her what she wants," they said, "because she is shouting after us." Evidently, they were not aware of his dilemma. "I was sent only to the lost sheep of the House of Israel," he explained. If he was quite sure of that, if he knew for certain he was not sent to heal non-Jews, why did he not send her away at once? That silence indicates genuine uncertainty. A new dimension of the Father's will had suggested itself, but he was not sure about the implication of the request. The woman, however, was quite sure of what she wanted. His silence had affected her; she recognized an element not provided for in the Messiah script, a genuine human hesitation before a difficult decision. She did not know what the difficulty was, but instead of the appeal of Child to Parent ("Son of David, take pity on me!"), she addressed him Adult to Adult, though respectfully: "Lord, help me."

His reply has shocked liberal-minded people, it sounds so brutally rude and insensitive, addressed to a woman in a state of acute unhappiness about her sick child: "It is not fair to take the children's food and throw it to the house dogs." The woman was quite accustomed to the way Jews called pagans "dogs," and anyway Jews used a word meaning pets rather than the wild scavengers of the streets. But there must have been something more than this to make her feel that the Jewish Teacher was not actually rejecting her. Hers was a "game" reply, it was what Berne calls a "switch" from the "proper" response, which would have been an abject groveling. She evidently felt this "switch" was in order, or she would not have thus thrown away her one hope of a cure by being impertinent to a stern and capricious Messiah. This means that Jesus' remark was evidently a "game" one, but it was a pretend game, because it is not remotely in character to suppose he would actually humiliate an already suffering human being. He simply thought she could give him the answer to his problem, so he "put on" the Messiah part for a minute to see what reaction it got.

> She retorted, "Ah yes, sir; but even house dogs can eat the scraps that fall from their master's table." Then Jesus answered her, "Woman, you have great faith. Let your wish be granted." And from that moment her daughter was well again. [Mt. 15:27–28]

The woman played the game of "poor little me," tongue-in-cheek. She knew perfectly well that the real dialogue was Adult to Adult and that the answer was "Yes." It was a "Yes" to Jesus' own self-questioning, too. And because

she, too, had discarded game-playing and made her real
request "straight," Jesus said she had "faith," i.e., she was
responding from out of her real self to his real self, and
they met in that incandescent moment of revelation of the
ultimate Self. This is a marvelous story, once its significance is disentangled, because it shows both a brisk, effective use of P.A.C. at two levels: to break a script and communicate "straight." It also shows the fact that once this is
done something more can follow, for love, imprisoned and
gagged by the script, is suddenly free to shoot heaven-
wards and break not only individual script hangups but
the "cosmic script" of sin which binds men and women in
ignorance, sickness, and despair.

But one could go on and on quoting. Jesus spent his
whole public life breaking scripts, and when he could not
get through to the Adult to do that, he could at least break
up the destructive games with which the unconverted
were trying to stop his work. Perhaps the best story of all,
is the tale in John, Chapter 9, of the man born blind who,
having been healed and totally converted himself (in an
eccentric and unexpected way that utterly routed his own
little games) went on to an uproarious session of game-
smashing with the Pharisees, which he clearly enjoyed a
lot, at their expense. So they threw him out of the religious
games-racket altogether (this was the worst thing they
could think of), and Jesus came and found him and received his (now utterly serious) profession of faith. The
man said, "Lord, I believe," and worshiped him. Jesus'
comment, as John recounts it, was:

> It is for judgment
> that I have come into this world,
> so that those without sight may see
> and those with sight turn blind.

"We are not blind, surely?" asked the Pharisees indig-
nantly when they heard about this, and his reply was as

ruthless as all his game-smashing remarks. He pulled them sharply off the Parent perch from which they wanted to conduct the argument and told it straight:

Blind? If you were,
you would not be guilty, [i.e., if you knew and acknowl-
    edged your lack of vision you could be helped]
but since you say "We see,"
your guilt remains.

"I am the light of the world," Jesus told them, and those who see the light can then radiate it themselves and show up the shabby prison-games for what they are, as the ex-blind man did. To analyze the whole account here is unnecessary, but to reread the story with these terms in mind is a revealing experience.

But more than individual conversions and healings was needed to break the Devil's cosmic script. In the end, Jesus, by his death, smashed the Messiah script and all the "worldly" Parent-type plans of salvation. Afterwards, his followers realized that it did, in fact, fit into the great pattern of God's design for the world he loved so much. At the time it did not make sense, and when the possibility first loomed up, Peter told Jesus to stop indulging in defeatist fantasies, or words to that effect. Jesus, who loved him dearly, thereupon called him "Satan" and told him his reactions were not "of God" but of men—that is, scripty ones, like the earlier suggestions from the Prince of Darkness. For he saw more and more clearly that in order to break the hold of sin and death, it was necessary to refuse to accept the assumptions about them being the ultimate, inevitable power. The Puer Aeternus, the natural Child, could only reopen Paradise by proving the ultimate powerlessness of evil. That meant letting it do its worst.

It is impossible for us to know clearly how Jesus, intellectually, understood the death-salvation doctrine. It was implicit in the spirituality and history of his people, espe-

cially in the words of the prophet Isaiah, who saw the role
of God's people, Israel, as the suffering servant of the
Lord, who would mysteriously bring salvation from sin, by
suffering its effects willingly:

> . . . a thing despised and rejected by men,
> a man of sorrows and familiar with suffering,
> a man to make people screen their faces;
> he was despised and we took no account of him.
> And yet ours were the sufferings he bore,
> ours the sorrows he carried.
> But we, we thought of him as someone punished,
> struck by God, and brought low.
> Yet he was pierced through for our faults,
> crushed for our sins.
> On him lies the punishment that brings us peace,
> and through his wounds we are healed. [Isa. 53:3–5]

It seems certain that Jesus thought deeply about this
passage, yet its application to himself was not necessarily
clear-cut, as it now seems to us after centuries of Christian
usage. On the other hand, he did undoubtedly know that
his script-breaking activities had roused the Parent in his
enemies to a dangerous pitch of vindictive rage. They
were scared of a rebellion by the Child in themselves, and
in the people who should have remained docile under
their Parental command, and they were determined to
crush that Child. Certainly, unless he changed his tac-
tics—and that he could not do—there was only one end to
the matter. The only question was when. It all came to a
head at the time of the great Passover pilgrimage to Jerusalem, partly because with Jerusalem packed with pilgrims,
the authorities were even more nervous than usual about
the possibility of a riot among the people if Jesus stirred
them up. Being scripty people themselves, they could not
help judging Jesus' actions according to that standard.
They still expected him to act out the Messiah script, only

from their point of view it was the wrong kind of Messiah.

Knowing what was to be expected, Jesus spent one last evening with his friends and celebrated a meal with them. It may or may not have been the actual Passover meal, but in any case it had a Passover significance in Jesus' mind. It linked the symbols of the Exodus—God's liberation of Israel, this Child, from the slavery of the Egyptian Parent—to the more fundamental liberation of mankind from sin and death. The ritual meal in which he endowed bread and wine with the meaning of his own body and blood signified that somehow or other his voluntary undergoing of the suffering caused by sin would also be their liberation, by "incorporating" them in himself. "The blood of the covenant," he called it, the sign of God's peace treaty with man. We cannot tell how much actually was said on that night by Jesus and how much is the work of informed memory picking up the significant point, dropping the irrelevant. The Gospel accounts are art, not tape-recording—the creation of the loving, responsive Child, not the "taken-down-in-evidence-against-you" of the Parent. So we have what matters, what he meant to, and did, convey. And what he conveyed in word and sign was acted out in brutal fact next day.

It was not the ritual death of a God-King but a political execution of one more disturber of the Parent-peace, which is spiritual death. Because Jesus had no script, and never had had one, it made sense for him to die. He died freely, not according to a dramatic necessity created by someone else. He would not play games, even when he was facing death. The chief priests tried to get him to join in a game of "I'm only trying to help you," but he simply would not answer. Then he had told them "straight" what he now knew about his own position in God's plan, adding sadly, "You will not believe me." They did not, of course, but they merely incorporated that saying in a new game— "Now he tells me!" they cried. Pilate tried the same game and also got nowhere. He was so impressed and startled that he actually talked "straight" to the crowd, in an attempt to get Jesus off, but the Parent had been working on the "little Fascist" in the crowd, and Pilate was too frightened by it to persist. His Adult was not strong enough, and he gave in.

The last word of Jesus sums up the whole matter. The Father to whom Jesus had always prayed, whose will he did, was never the Father-Parent, whether kind and indulgent or stern and vengeful. He was the Life-giver, the Source and Self of man, from which Jesus had "come forth" to be the explicit, recognizable script-breaking Word of power. So at the end, there was nothing to separate him from that life. "Father, into your hands I commit my spirit." And that Spirit was the one that had spoken the words of healing and freedom to so many. It was the Spirit he bequeathed to his lovers for evermore, to do the same work of healing and regeneration, as he told Nicodemus: "Unless a man is born from above he cannot enter the Kingdom of God," and that rebirth he underwent and made possible for those who, recognizing him, said "yes" to the Spirit. "As the Father sent me, so I am sending you," he told the disciples after he had risen.

His rising was simply the natural consequence of what he was. He was one over whom death and sin had no power, because they had never "taken hold" on his self. He knew them, lived with them, argued and fought with them, suffered under them, and died—but that ultimate Self, the Spirit that is of the Father, could not die, because it simply is not that kind of thing.

And having proved that sin and death are the ultimate sick game played by the Devil, he was in a position to show others how to break up that game, too. As Paul put it:

> When we were baptised we went into the tomb with him and joined him in death, so that as Christ was raised from the dead by the Father's glory, we too might live a new life. . . . Death has no power over

him any more. When he died, he died, once for all, to
sin, so his life now is life with God; and in that way,
you too must consider yourselves to be dead to sin but
alive for God in Christ Jesus. [Rom. 6:4, 9–11]

Of course, as we have seen, the angry, defrauded Parent
is still hanging around looking for a chance to wreck
things. But still, the "permission" to stop belonging to
death has been given. It needs support and "follow-up"
and lots of explanation and help, but the cure is available,
the work of healing is begun. Only it has to be done the
way he did it:

The wounded surgeon plies the steel
That questions the distempered part;
Beneath the bleeding hands we feel
The sharp compassion of the healer's art
Resolving the enigma of the fever chart.

Our only health is the disease
If we obey the dying nurse
Whose constant care is not to please
But to remind of our, and Adam's curse,
And that, to be restored, our sickness must grow worse.
                    [T. S. Eliot, *The Four Quartets*]

We still like to think we do not need this drastic cure,
that we are really quite well ("We are not blind, surely?")
and real, and it is only "circumstances" that are wrong.
(Berne calls this scapegoat "Arsisiety"—a familiar bogey
among discontented script-ridden people.) But Eliot reminds us that there really is only one way out, that we can
take it, and that we *know* it is the right way, even when
we reject it:

The dripping blood our only drink,
The bloody flesh our only food:

In spite of which we like to think
That we are sound, substantial flesh and blood—
Again, in spite of that, we call this Friday good.

That is where the mystics come in. Not all men are called
to the mystic way, but the mystics know more about the
way to which Jesus calls all men than most of us do. Being
undistracted by desires for the "stroking" of the Parent,
they know a cheat when they see one, and keep on telling
us both that the world and people and love and bodies and
trees and waves and even machines are beautiful, and that
if we hang onto them we shall never find out what they
have to tell us. But the greatest cheat of all is the idea that
we become more ourselves when we grab things or people
or our own qualities and abilities. Thomas Merton, who
ended up a saint as well as a mystic, put it to men and
women of our time, and he put it straight. He was never
one to play pious games:

> It was because the saints were absorbed in God that
> they are truly capable of seeing and appreciating
> created things, and it was because they loved him
> alone that they alone loved everybody.
>   The saint knows that the world and everything
> made by God is good, while those who are not saints
> either think that created things are unholy, or else
> they don't bother about the question . . . because
> they are only interested in themselves.
>   Resting in his glory above all pleasure and pain, joy
> or sorrow, and every other good or evil, we love in all
> things his will rather than the things themselves, and
> that is why we make creation a sacrifice in praise of
> God.
>   The only true joy on earth is to escape from the
> prison of our own self-hood [he means not the Self
> where we touch God but the "selfish" self, the device
> which is a response to a world of "sin"—interior and

exterior shades of the prison house] and enter by love into union with the Life who dwells and sings within the essence of every creature, and in the core of our own souls. [*Seeds of Contemplation*]

The message is the same as that of the great Hindu and Buddhist mystical tradition, and at the end of his life Merton himself discovered more and more deeply the "Christian" value of that tradition, but there is one difference, and it is crucial. The Eastern mystic could talk of "the Life which dwells . . . in the core of our souls," but for the Christian mystic it is a person, it is "the Life *who* dwells" in the heart that is open to him. God can set free any man or woman, anywhere, any time, but Jesus is the "Word" about how it happens, he is, to recall the earlier chapters of this book, the "language" of God's therapy for a sick world. And, as we saw, the effectiveness of the development *after* conversion depends on the power and accuracy of the language we use to understand what has happened. The saving "language" of God is the "Word" who says "I came that you might have life and have it more abundantly." As Paul put it, in startlingly contemporary terms:

The Son of God, the Christ Jesus that we proclaimed to you . . . was never Yes and No: with him it was always Yes, and however many the promises God made, the Yes to them all is in him. That is why it is "through him" that we answer Amen to the praise of God. [II Cor. 1:19–20]

"God thinks you're O.K." We have to know that, and act on it. That is the beginning, without which nothing else can happen. After that, anything can happen. Pentecost, for instance, when timid disciples were suddenly able to go out and preach, facing prison, beatings, and eventually death, because the Spirit of Jesus had taken them over. It still happens. This was written only a few years ago, by a

man who had been a sincere Christian for years but found
that conversion was only the beginning. He discovered
what it was all about through the experience of the same
Spirit that swept through Peter and the others.

> We have found ourselves on a plane of Christian life
> all the text books call normal and all practice and ex-
> pectation seem to deny. Our faith has come alive, our
> believing has become a kind of knowing. Jesus Christ
> is a real person to us, a real living person who is our
> Lord and who is active in our lives. . . . A love of
> Scriptures . . . a transformation of our relationships
> with others, a need and a power to witness beyond all
> expectation, have all become part of our lives.

But it is not feelings or ecstasies or visions that make
that Word sing in the heart and transform it. These can
show what it is all about, they are so strange and so full of
glory, but still what the author of the *Cloud of Unknowing*
calls "this work" has to be done in times of depression and
discouragement, in the "dark night of the soul." Another
mystic, Walter Hilton, said firmly:

> And though it be so that thou feel him in devotion or
> in knowing, or in any other gift whatever it be, rest not
> there as though thou hadst fully found Jesus, but
> forget what thou hast found and always be desiring
> after Jesus more and more to find him better. . . . For
> wit thou well that what thou feelest of him, be it never
> so much . . . yet hast thou not found Jesus as he is in
> his joy.

It all happens on the journey, which begins with the
joyful, liberated Child. But the Child is easily self-ab-
sorbed, taken up with that private happiness. He has to
recognize also that love in his own "core" is not at all

private but is the place where he touches the Self, who is the Self of others, too: Julian of Norwich knew this:

> It is God's will that I see myself as much bound to him in love as if he had done for *me* all that he hath done, and thus should every soul think inwardly of her Lover. That is to say, the Charity of God maketh in us such a unity that, when it is truly seen, no man can part himself from others.

This "owing" of man to God is also the "owing" of man to man, so that, as God says to the person, "You're O.K.," and the person hears, and is set free, so each liberated Child should speak out to those still in prison, and say, "I'm O.K.—you're O.K.—this is true because God says so!" We can see it happening, but we do not know exactly how it works. It is beyond the limits of language, which is where the real things are done.

> There is a great Deed that our Lord shall do [wrote Julian of Norwich] in which Deed he shall save his word [i.e., do as he promised or "covenanted"] and shall make all well that is not well. How it shall be done there is no creature beneath Christ that knoweth it, nor shall know it till it is done. . . . It shall be worshipful and marvellous and plenteous and God himself shall do it; and this shall be the highest joy that may be, to behold the Deed that God himself shall do. . . .

And so "all shall be well, and all manner of things shall be well," and this is not a jolly optimism to cover up real sin and death, but the assertion that God's work is greater than anything that sin can do. The Child who came from God's hand, still trailing a cloudy garment of that glory for which he was made, is beset by enemies, battered, ca-

joled, and deceived. But he is not alone. The Word of
freedom is spoken to him, in all kinds of ways, and he has
a growing Adult that can hear it and understand it and
open the door for the Child to come out. After that calling
begins a long journey to which we are drawn by love. It is
the journey to Paradise, but not a going backwards, for the
first Paradise is the innocence of the unformed and hopeful. When we get to where we are going we shall be
changed by the journey—still the Child, but complete, ful-
filled, whole. Paradise is regained through fire, as Pascal
and so many others have said, and that fire purifies, trans-
forms, and perfects. It is also through the water of death
and cleansing and rebirth, for Jesus said we should be
reborn of water and the Holy Spirit, whose sign is the
tongues of flame. Yet it is all, somehow, homely and familiar:

With the drawing of that Love and the voice of this Calling
We shall not cease from exploration
And the end of our exploring
Will be to arrive where we started
And know the place for the first time.
Through the unknown, remembered gate
When the last of earth left to discover
Is that which was the beginning;
At the source of the longest river
The voice of the hidden waterfall
And the children in the apple-tree
Not known, because not looked for
But heard, half-heard, in the stillness
Between two waves of the sea.
Quick now, here, now, always—
A condition of complete simplicity
(Costing not less than everything)
And all shall be well and
All manner of thing shall be well
When the tongues of flame are in-folded

Into the crowned knot of fire
And the fire and the rose are one.
[T. S. Eliot, *The Four Quartets*]

Complete simplicity—yet the complex rose is the symbol of wholeness, the mandala flower, expressing the unity
of life. The fire makes all one (but it costs no less than everything). The complexities and struggles of a lifetime of
searching for God fall away, in the end, to complete simplicity, the Child is taken home.

But what of those who have never heard the word that
liberates, or, having heard it, dared not respond, because
the cost is "not less than everything"? We cannot know,
but we do know from the record of those famous "death-
bed repentances," which cynics take to be proof of the hypocrisy of religious faith, that the imminence of death is a
powerful script-breaker. Death is real, and it makes the
play-acting of a "scripted" life show up for what it is.
There is, indeed, a very old Christian belief that God gives
to every man that "last chance," even if there is no evidence of it that others can see:

Between the stirrup and the ground
He mercy sought and Mercy found.

More than that we cannot say, except that Christ is
Lord of death, and to say "No" then means to say a deliberate "No" to that Love and that Calling. It must be a very
great hatred that does that.

In any case, at the end, not only the elaborate structures
of the script, but even the wise decisions and achievements of the enlightened Adult fall away. There is only
the Child, alone, afraid, but confident in the Father's love.

When she lay dying, Elizabeth Fry—reformer, preacher,
adviser of kings and governments, friend of the oppressed,
wife and mother and grandmother—opened her eyes after
long hours of silence. She had been alone in those hours,

although surrounded by loving comforters. She had been alone with the fear of death, which had haunted her all her life, and she had been alone with God. Outside the window, the waves of the sea roared onto the beach, the waves she had so dreaded when she was a little girl. And it was the little girl, Betsy Gurney of Norfolk, who spoke at last, to the maid, Mary, using the speech she must have picked up in babyhood from a nurse, with an old Norse word incorporated into the speech of the country people who lived where once the Vikings had settled. "Strift" means oppression, struggle, the pain of life, the battle with evil, which is never over until death. But for Betsy the struggle was ending in victory, and her Child rejoiced, as she went home:

Oh Mary, Mary—it is strift—but I am safe!

Notes on Sources

CHAPTER 1

Berg, Leila. *Look at Kids*. Baltimore, Md.: Penguin, 1972.
Confessions of St. Augustine. Translated by F. J. Sheed. New York: Sheed and Ward, 1969.
Godden, Rumer. *An Episode of Sparrows*. London: Macmillan, 1956.
Golding, William. *Lord of the Flies*. New York: Putnam, 1959.
"Journals of Elizabeth Fry." Unpublished manuscript in the Library of the Society of Friends, Euston Road, London.
Killilea, M. *Karen*. Englewood Cliffs, N.J.: Prentice-Hall, 1962.
Lewis, C. S. *The Voyage of the "Dawn Treader"* (Book 3 in the Chronicles of Narnia). New York: Macmillan, 1952.
———. *The Silver Chair* (Book 4 in the Chronicles of Narnia). New York: Macmillan, 1953.
Lewis, Eve. *The Psychology of Family Religion*. London: Sheed and Ward, 1968.

CHAPTER 2

Berne, Eric. *What Do You Say After You Say Hello?* New York: Grove, 1972.
Frank, Anne. *The Diary of a Young Girl*. Garden City, New York: Doubleday, 1952.

Greene, Graham. *End of the Affair.* London: William Heinemann, 1951.
Lewis, Oscar. *The Children of Sanchez.* New York: Random House, 1961.
Marshall, Catherine. *Christy.* New York: McGraw-Hill, 1967.
Mortimer, Ernest. *Blaise Pascal.* New York: Humanities Press, 1959.

CHAPTER 3

Bhagavad Gita. Translated by Juan Mascaro. Baltimore, Md.: Penguin, 1962.
Bonhoeffer, Dietrich. *The Cost of Discipleship.* London: SCM, 1959.
Cruz, Nicky. *Run, Baby, Run; The Story of a Gang-Lord Turned Crusader.* Plainfield, N.J.: Logos, 1968.
Eliade, Mircea. *Myths, Dreams, and Mysteries.* New York: Harper and Row, 1960.
Eliot, T. S. *Murder in the Cathedral.* London: Faber and Faber, 1947.
Gray, Francine du Plessis. *Divine Disobedience.* New York: Knopf, 1970.
Lepp, Ignace. *From Karl Marx to Jesus Christ.* London: Sheed and Ward, 1959.
Moorhouse, Geoffrey. *Against All Reasons.* New York: Stein and Day, 1969.
Tolkien, J. R. R. "On Fairy Stories," *Tree and Leaf.* London: George Allen and Unwin, 1964.
Trapp, Maria A. *The Story of the Trapp Family Singers.* Philadelphia: Lippincott, 1949.
Vann, Gerald. *Water and the Fire.* New York: Sheed and Ward, 1954.
Wilkerson, David. *Born Old.* Grand Rapids, Mich.: Zondervan.

CHAPTER 4

Berne, Eric. *What Do You Say After You Say Hello?* New York: Grove, 1972.
Bhagavad Gita. Translated by Juan Mascaro. New York: Penguin, 1962.
Buddhist Scriptures. Translated by E. Conye. New York: Penguin, 1971.
Eliade, Mircea. *Myths, Dreams, and Mysteries.* New York: Harper and Row, 1960.
Martin, P. W. *Experiment in Depth.* London: Routledge, 1956.
Merton, Thomas. *Conjectures of a Guilty Bystander.* Garden City, New York: Doubleday, 1968.
Sackville-West, V. *The Eagle and the Dove.* Garden City, New York: Doubleday, 1944.

CHAPTER 5

Eliot, T. S. *Four Quartets.* London: Faber and Faber, 1944.
Merton, Thomas. *Seeds of Contemplation.* London: Burns and Oates, 1960.

ACKNOWLEDGMENTS

Grateful acknowledgment is extended to the following publishers for permission to quote from the copyrighted material listed:

From *Murder In The Cathedral* by T. S. Eliot, copyright, 1935, by Harcourt Brace Jovanovich, Inc.; copyright, 1963, by T. S. Eliot. Reprinted by permission of Harcourt Brace Jovanovich, Inc., and Faber and Faber Ltd.

From "East Coker" in *Four Quartets* by T. S. Eliot, copyright, 1943, by T. S. Eliot; copyright, 1971, by Esme Valerie Eliot. Reprinted by permission of Harcourt Brace Jovanovich, Inc., and Faber and Faber Ltd.

From "Little Gidding" in *Four Quartets* by T. S. Eliot, copyright, 1943, by T. S. Eliot; copyright, 1971, by Esme Valerie Eliot. Reprinted by permission of Harcourt Brace Jovanovich, Inc., and Faber and Faber Ltd.

From *The Cost Of Discipleship,* 2nd ed., by Dietrich Bonhoeffer, © SCM Press Ltd. 1959. Condensed with permission of Macmillan Publishing Co., Inc., and SCM Press Ltd.

From *The Story Of The Trapp Family Singers* by Maria Augusta Trapp. Copyright 1949 by Maria Augusta Trapp. Reprinted by permission of J. B. Lippincott Company.

From *An Episode Of Sparrows* by Rumer Godden. Reprinted by permission of Macmillan London and Basingstoke.

From *The End Of The Affair* by Graham Greene. Reprinted by permission of William Heinemann, Ltd.

From *Pity My Simplicity* by P. E. Sangster. Reprinted by permission of the Epworth Press.